Voices In A Crowd

Edited by

Sarah Marshall

First published in Great Britain in 2004 by
ANCHOR BOOKS
Remus House,
Coltsfoot Drive,
Peterborough, PE2 9JX
Telephone (01733) 898102

All Rights Reserved

Copyright Contributors 2003

SB ISBN 1 84418 300 9

To Melanie,

I will Love you until the seas run dry and time stands still. xx

Foreword

Anchor Books is a small press, established in 1992, with the aim of promoting readable poetry to as wide an audience as possible.

We hope to establish an outlet for writers of poetry who may have struggled to see their work in print.

The poems presented here have been selected from many entries, and as always editing proved to be a difficult task.

I trust this selection will delight and please the authors and all those who enjoy reading poetry.

Sarah Marshall
Editor

CONTENTS

Julie	Sharon Spencer	1
Freshly Caught Today	Eric Ferris	2
Music	P P Christodoulides	3
The Tree Of Knowledge	M J Banasco	4
Our Problems To God	Catherine Woo Yen Yee	5
Blind Alley	Alan Millard	6
Extraction	Martin McMackin	7
Dog In The Window	Donald Linnett	8
Old Faithful	Sid 'de' Knees	9
Her Secret Place	R Mills	10
Elephant Man	Greta Robinson	11
The Lady In The Old Town	Mandy Jayne Moon	12
Conversation With A Dead Man!	Roy Angus Millar	13
Keep Faith	Philip Naylor	13
House Of Despair	Adrian Salamon	14
Falling Stars	Emma Scott	15
Where Did All The Industry Go?	Jennifer Austin	16
Nature And Me	Ian Fisher	16
Here Again	Anne Davey	17
Rest Assured	Joan Prentice	17
A Young Man Dying	David M Walford	18
Fenland Law	Richard Pollington	19
More To Share	Louise Keene	20
A Poet's Life	Peter Mahoney	21
The Unforgettable 11 09 2001	Kopan Mahadeva	22
Life	Katie Davies	23
Wakey . . . Wakey!	F R Smith	24
Gravestones	David Light	25
The Parks of Oxford City	The Warrior Poet - Eamon John Healy	26
Half Term	G Siddall	27
Comfortably Broke!	Matt Riley	28
Sleep	Ricky N Lock	29
Rags To Riches	Gillian Humphries	30
The Dog	Roy Kimpton	31
Remembrance	Suzanne Thorne	32

Title	Author	Page
Dawn	Sheila Cheesman	32
Winter's Woe	Eddie Main	33
It Seems	Eileen Stuart	33
Remember Them At Christmas	Rachel Ford	34
On The Death Of A Seafaring Brother	Jean-Angela Smith	34
Being A Knee	Emma Scott	35
Dallas	James Patrick Milton	35
A Truthful Hanging	Shaw o'Inchrory	36
Birdsong	Jon El Wright	37
Friendship	Carol Hanney	38
Freedom	Mick Vick	38
Dust Upon The Winds Of Time	Vladimir Nikolai Vetchinsky	39
January Sales	Jacqueline O'nions	39
Tombstones In Bottesford Churchyard	Ray Smart	40
Charity Shops	Mary Hill	41
Links	Chris Creedon	42
The Flower And The Firework	P Brewer	43
Carol Ann	Carol Ann Darling	44
?	D Roberts	45
Eeh! By Gum!	Mary Skelton	46
Mystery Man	Sheila Benard	47
My Walk	May Ward	47
Unholy Spirit	Douglas Bryan Kennett	48
From Greece To England	Joyce Gee	49
The Flu Jab	Lachlan Taylor	50
My Message	C S Cyster	51
Who Am I?	O A Oshinbolu	52
To Step Outside	Linda Chapman	53
A Tiny Step Towards Tomorrow	Jo Lodge	54
Death Of A Princess	Teresa Kilcullen-Davies	54
With You	Sue Tobin	55
Flowers In Bloom	Rosemary Davies	55
My Grandma	Jil Moorehead	56
Blue Angels	Patricia Carter	57
Liar's Building	Oliver Pickerin	58
The Stillbirth	Anna Yates	59

A Family Lost In Time	Colin Allsop	60
The Old Fighter	Peter Haines	61
One For The Road	T G Bloodworth	62
Ah To Be Young Again!	David A Bray	62
Fame 2003	Derek B Hewertson	63
The Citizen's Charter	Christopher Higgins	64
Happy And Pity	John Belcher	65
My First Big Bike	Alan Adcock	66
Time, Space	Dennis L Vasey	67
Time Capsule	Opal Innsbruk	68
Goddess Of The Moon	Denis Martindale	69
A Lover's Heart	Shane Quinn	70
Trust	Maria Jenkinson	71
I'll Be There For You	Helen Carpenter	72
The Old Mine	Geoffrey Leech	73
New Baby	Richard Trowbridge	74
Allegorising Life	C Thornton	74
An Ill Wind Blow Through ... Yoga!	J M Hefti Whitney	75
Tribute To My Neighbours	Ivy Lott	76
Grandma's Story	Carol Ann Awdas	76
Another Sunrise	Dave Austin	77
No Rhyme Or Reason	Ruth Markinson	77
Glee Castle	Nick Clifton	78
The Past Revisited	Isobel Laffin	79
Nation How Trust?	John J Flint	80
In His Time	George Reed	81
Never Test Unconditional Love	Graham Hare	82
Cradle Song	Stephen Forward	83
The Move	Muriel Johnson	84
Book Week Assembly At Robert Peel Lower School	Doreen Lawrence	85
Nature's Ghost	Rose Murdoch	86
He	Sharon Grimer	87
Shake Hands With Billy Reid	John Marshall	88
Remember Schoolmates	Jack Edwards	89
Selective Hearing	Anne Gardiner	90
Bramble Bush	Alan Pow	91

Comparing You To The Weather	Parveen K Saini	92
Old-Age Misery	Mandy Lee	92
My Little Dog	BJ	93
Truth	M Lane	94
In My Eyes	P Allen	94
Retired!	Frances Ridett	95
No Oxygen Room	Jennifer Edwards	95
The Witches	Leslie Tomlinson	96
Peter	Anita Cooling	97
The Silence!	Alan Vann	98
Nine/Eleven	Jenny Hitchen	98
My Terra-Nova	Brenda Nicholson	99
Ride Your Horse	Keith L Powell	99
Brittlebank Farm	A F Mace	100
Evening Star	Hazel Mills	101
Essentials	Lyn Sandford	101
My Special Friend	Megan Strong	102
Mother's Day	Rebecca Bamford	102
Test In Life	Reimunda Jones	103
The Drunk	Florence M Bullen	104
The River Leen	R Martin	105
Relief	Helen Trevatt	106
Matelots	Andrew Vaughan	106
An Old-Fashioned Christmas	Jan Ross	107
The Brookedale Club	Sharon Tremlett	108
Infertility	Jillian Shields	109
All Alone	I K Skinner	110
The Tramp	Maureen Turner	110
Neighbours?	Dan Pugh	111
Trick-Or-Treat!	Roger Williams	112
Nothing Better To Do!	Geraldine McMullan Doherty	112
That Autumn Time Of Year	M Strong	113
Animal Angst	Martine Jane Meah	113
Nan	Justin Stonell	114
The Snow Queen	P McIntyre	115
Hallowe'en	Parveen K Saini	115
The Law Of The Kitchen	Albert E Bird	116
Have You Ever	A M Owen	117

Wishes	H K Banks	118
The Zoo	Claire Bloor	118
Seaside Science	Maureen Keeble	119
Not In My Back Yard	Kim Montia	119
Mother	Keith Bennett	120
The Silent Scream	Jeanette Jackson	121
Expendable	Amy McLaughlan	122
A Different World	Ali Collins	122
A Plea For Help	Lydia Barnett	123
Final Destination	Lindsay Kelly	124
The Witch	Lottie Dolby	125
The Umbrella Of Life	Maryska Carson	126
The Sea	Linda Davies	127
Stu's Curry	Nicola Cobham	127
A Blessing For Lizzie	P Carleton	128
Silly Rhyme	K Horsnell	129
Stress	B Foster	130
Reminders	S Cuthbert	131
Hoping For The Robin's Return	Donna June Clift	132
Sunday At My Gran's	Stephen Frederick Burns	133
The Butterfly . . .	Janet Brook	134
I'm Sorry	John Lee	134
Morning After 2	Jane England	135
I Woke But Did I?	Maria Jayne Halliday	136
Perspective	Mary Frances Mooney	137
Of Aztecs And Conquistadors	Juan Pablo Jalisco	138
Elver Harvest	Martin Blakemore Davis	139
Nature's Blessings	Henry Crawford	140
For My Honey	Daniel Jones Jr	141
The Silvered Glassy Sea	Ian C Gray	142
Eternal Eye Of Gibraltar	Anthony M Blackwell	143
River Tyne	Les Davey	144
Untitled	D G Douglas	144
Sistine Sonnet	Bill Looker	145
Mother	Garth Evans	145
Memories	I Horwell	146
Doctor's Surgery	Marilyn Hine	147
The Old Car Boot	Ella Wright	147

Title	Author	Page
Was God A Time Traveller	Walter Mottram	148
My Daddy	S P Cockayne	149
Redundancy	L Alan Johnson	150
Belonging - The Way We Are	Jo Allen	151
Untitled	Jacky Edwards	152
Mission To Mars	Maureen Carr	153
A Friday Walk	Trevor Headley	154
Save Our Tree	Ann M Crampton	155
Holiday Island	Eileen Robinson	156
The Love	D Salter	156
Stoke On Where?	Steve Rushton	157
Rainbows	Helen McLellan	157
Our Wonderful Countryside	Richard Trezise	158
The Potteries	Steve Jervis-Price	159
The Phantom	Peter W Hodgkins	160
My Soul	Kay Hope	161
A Look At Life	W Kershaw	161
Lost Then Found	Jean Hargreaves	162
The Bag Lady	Jane Hewitt	163
Images M	Victor Church	164
Butterfly Tree	Joe Wood	164
Be Mine	Carol Mary Woods	165
My Pride, My Joy	Mary McKeeve Moore	166
Janling Sichel	Brian Dilworth	167
A Ring Around The Basin	Wendy Smith	168
Perhaps I Should Have Spoken Up Sooner	A G Revill	169
Freedom	Saleem Tariq	169
My Dream	Gerald T Western	170
Modern And Ancient - Continued	Nell Thompson	170
Building On Belief	Linda Preece	171
She	Charlene Soan	172
Arrived At Last	J V Waby	173
The Church That Moved	Doug Sheppard	174
The Writer's Journey	Beverley J Todd	175
Be Grateful	Lois Taylor	176
The Cuckoo	Susan Roden	177
A Gem Of A County	Peter Parbery	178

Hope	Chris Needley	178
To Bare . . . Or Not	Wendy Watkin	179
Scents	Nigel Sinkins	180
An Open Eye	Rebecca Timothy	181
Rejection	Robert Joseph Parks	182
Woman With Carrots	Antony Sheaman	183
Farewell To Love	Patricia Samuels	184
Annie's Door	Denise Shaw	184
Changing By Nature . . .	Louise Webster	185
The Knock Out	George Petrie	186
Arctic Underworld	Ann Odger	187
Only A Game	Beatrice M Wilson	188
To A Faery-Thorn Seen In A Field In Ireland	Gardiner M Weir	188
Essex	Denise Ryan	189
Darkness	Cassius James	189
A Meeting At The Cenotaph The Miracle At . . .	June Pledger	190
Turning Clocks Back!	C R Slater	191
A Summer's Day	Tracey Stanton	192
The Genesis Story	Jonathan Pegg	193
By Chance	Ray Racy	194
Someone, I Wish	B Page	195
Take Me!	Nikki Raven	196
Love Reunited	Marj Busby	197
Anyone Can Write Poetry	Patricia Adele Draper	198
Adversity	Michelle Rae	198
Autumn Revelation	Anthony J Brady	199
I Love You Still	Tonya M Barber	200
Invisible Man	Peter Wesley Hayward	201
Poppies	Stephanie Pereira	202
When I Write	Sian Marie Mernor	203
Single Rose	Cindy Cross	203
Daemon Flu	Tom Ritchie	204
Farewell	Irene Keeling	206
Old Mother Earth	A C Small	206
How We Lived	Margaret Upson	207
Desolation Planet Earth	Ann G Wallace	208

All Grown Up	Jill K Gilbert	209
The Knowledge	Lorraine Noble	210
Daughters	J T Lister	210
A Forest Glade	Alan Morgan	211
Terrible Twos	L Fritchley	212
Lady Moon	Pauline Stevens	213
Mine Eyes	John Henry Stafford	214
Golden	Joyce Lawrence	215
My Single Beautiful Rose	Jenny Plant	216
Catch Me If You Can	R N Taber	217
Success	C King	218
Celebrity Hotel	Suzan Gumush	219
Big Strong Boys	E Dunn	220
'Die' Heat	Gloria B Rogers	221
Why Am I Here?	Marion Schoeberlein	222
He Walks With Me	Sam Ambrose	223
Another Vietnam	S Farley	223
Be Still	Joan May Wills	224
It's My Life	J Stone	225
A Mother's Lament	Emma M Gascoyne	226

JULIE
*(Dedicated to my beautiful granddaughter, Julie
24th May 2002 - 21st October 2003)*

The light in our life's been extinguished,
Severe pain in our hearts won't subside.
There's nowhere that we can find solace,
Our heartbreak we cannot abide.

You left us when we weren't expecting,
We took you for granted back then.
Your love and your laughter enthralled us,
We'd die to secure your return.

Deprived of your cheeky demeanour,
We've all lost the will to move on.
The world seems so hostile and cold now,
Life's empty since you have been gone.

We pray that your parting was painless,
And that you're at peace up above.
We loved you so much, we adored you,
How shall we endure our great loss?

So if you're above and can hear us,
Please wait till our time here is done.
We want nothing more than to join you,
To bask in the warmth of your grin.

Sharon Spencer

FRESHLY CAUGHT TODAY

Ah, 'tis obvious the art of this prose,
Is to play to the end and then dispose,
But the artifice of this desperate rhyme,
Leaves me akimbo, like solemn slime:

Rest at ease, my doughty crew;
Interest will spread, aye you, and you!
As plots and fables slowly unfold,
From uncharted depths spring words of gold!

So put up your feet and rest awhile,
Sleep and slumber, drowse and smile.
It's not your duty to concentrate,
Give others the post, let them relate.

As long as this web site holds truer than true,
This poet at least, will remain with you.
A colourful jester, a Forward Press crew,
Fresh words picked daily from the azure blue.

Eric Ferris

MUSIC

Music is the complex
expressed in tone
and has the quality
to lull the soul.

When you are feeling sad
and need to be cheered up,
play some music, dance
or listen, say, to jazz.

Music is the art of arts
to the very heart of hearts
even beating chords
never strung before.

Classical music, on the other hand,
encapsulates all that is life at large,
nature's miracles and charms
humans' turmoil and loves.

What music to have?
Naturally choose the one
that suits the mood at hand!

P P Christodoulides

THE TREE OF KNOWLEDGE

Sheltered

When once a child I played in childish thoughts
I played with toys at childish games that only children wrought
I sheltered safe in innocence for silliness was my world
Where innocence was all my truth . . . for truth alone is real

My mind reached out . . . would bring this world to me
My eyes grew wide each dawn of day at all what's new I'd see
My fingers stretched and touched . . . so I could understand
As innocence did walk with me and gently held my hand

I spoke in childish words that only children speak
In innocence and wisdom reserved for me the meek
For innocence and wisdom are the playmates of the child
Imagined friends . . . that none can see . . . except the young and mild!

Climbed

When once a man I put aside child's thoughts
No longer played or smiled those silly games once sought
I climbed for knowledge . . . now learning was my world
For learning yet became my truth and proud did ask what's real?

My mind reached out . . . would bring this world to me
But eyes grew dim each dawn of day at all my soul did see
My fingers stretched and touched . . . yet did not understand
As knowledge walked with me and roughly held my hand

I spoke the adult words that only adults speak
In knowledge and in learning that pride alone does reek
For pride and human intellect are the demons of the man
Imagined friends . . . that none can see . . . except the wise that can!

Entangled

When once a little wise I though upon that child
The simple and the innocent that grew unkempt and wild
Who'd climb the tree of knowledge and tempted played the clown
Now I would give all I have learnt to turn and climb back down

And in these thoughts so musing I realised that this child
Though gone; remained, could pray this pride to mild
For prayer must be the footholds that I could tread to search
To trust again in innocence to inherit all the Earth

And should I gain this ground once more then let me teach my son
Nothing; for rather shall I lead him to walk though he would run
Into the light from shadows . . . guiding wary of that tree.
I once in Adam's garden climbed . . . where pride entangled me.

M J Banasco

OUR PROBLEMS TO GOD

When our problems and burdens are so hard to bear
Tears just flow out wishing for someone to share
That's when we realise none other than God who is there
For His love for us is beyond compare

Most of the time when things aren't smooth along the way
We try to struggle through but there seems to be no way
We blame God for being slow in such a way
God says, 'My child that's because you never let go in any way.'

When our lives no longer see the rainbow
When our self-esteem seems so low
God says, 'Give me your hand and I'll never let you go
For I will show you the way as you are more precious than gold.'

Catherine Woo Yen Yee

BLIND ALLEY

Sometimes I tire of myself, as though
I've lived inside the confines of my brain
and learned (just as a local grows to know
his town, and every inch of its terrain)
the shortcuts and the alleyways that lead
to where I've been a thousand times before
and will a thousand times again. I need
to break out of the cul-de-sac, explore
those strange, forbidden places that I dread,
travel where I've never been before
and trespass where I've never dared to tread;
there are mountains that I long to climb, and seas
I long to sail, horizons that conceal
new, unseen worlds that beckon me and tease
with all they long to offer and reveal,
but something holds me back and ties me down:
those secret alleyways, that hidden lane,
the trappings of this old, familiar town
whose long-established pathways are my brain.

Alan Millard

EXTRACTION

Dent. A mark that remains.
But once, too, a tooth?
Under the raw gum
Tender with growth

The jawbone of language retains
Memory in shape,
Canalised meaning,
An ancient bonescape.

A hollow, a mould,
Once womb of a new word,
Now old, licked loose
By a lifetime of tongue.

Probed to the threshold of pain
Nerve endings become never-endings, hum.
Umbilical strings stretched to a high tone,
Then severed to none.

Philological fruit
Chewed to the stone.
A word pulled out at the root,
From the bone.

Martin McMackin

DOG IN THE WINDOW

I'm the little nodding dog
In the car in front of you
As I look out of my window
There's not much of a view
All I see is you.

I'm the little nodding dog
And I'm feeling really blue
I'm stuck here on the sill
I just don't know what to do
I haven't got a clue.

I'm the little nodding dog
And when we go for a ride
I sit here all alone
With the windows open wide
All I want to do is hide.

I'm the little nodding dog
I've been sitting here for years
I've listened to the arguments
The laughter and the tears
If I could, I'd give three cheers.

I'm the little nodding dog
And all I see is where I've been
I never see where I'm going
Even though I'm really keen
The driver is too mean.

I'm the little nodding dog
Churchill is my name
I'm often on the telly
Insurance is my game
It's my only claim to fame.

I'm the little nodding dog
And I always bear the brunt
I'm fed up sitting in the back
So now I will be blunt . . .
'I want to sit up front!'

Donald Linnett

OLD FAITHFUL

So patiently I will wait for you,
With my arms open wide.
I'm loyal, honest, faithful, true,
And I love your backside.

You only visit me to serve,
To aid as you ache.
Some days I think you've such a nerve,
As you for granted take.

That I will always be on tap,
And always show I care.
But I'll not always take this crap,
Not always be your chair.

I may one day be firewood,
Or took up to the tip.
And then you'll miss me as you should,
When we can't share a kip.

Sid 'de' Knees

HER SECRET PLACE

Is this your place of rest
Of dreams' golden slumber
With love that's now gone
Your secret locked within?

Flowers are barring the way
So no one disturbs your rest
Those golden suns are forever
Set now in a burnished hue.

Rivers of blue, yellow and gold
Pass by you in your dreams
As you rest, no more to be seen
In your secret place you hide.

There, a waterfall that makes no sound.
Flowers never to be seen abound
There he stands, head turned in grief
As she sits upon her throne of coral.

Looking out at the golden sunset
In her secret place she found
She lets no one enter within
Only the secret to which she's bound.

R Mills

ELEPHANT MAN

Beauty's skin-deep.
How you longed for sleep,
but you couldn't lie down,
not even to weep.

Such beauty inside,
but you had to hide
and no one to care
if you lived or died.

A pathetic sight,
you hobbled through the night.
Half of you obeying,
the other, poised for flight.

You found a true friend,
surely now, pain must end,
but broken spirits
cannot easily mend.

What could you do?
No salvation for you.
They just could not see
you were beautiful too.

You sat on your bed,
sadly lay down your head.
The pillow felt good,
moments later, you were dead.

Greta Robinson

THE LADY IN THE OLD TOWN

Her name is Eileen Fowlie,
And she runs the Anchor pub,
So if you're feeling hungry
Get *Mo* to cook some grub
Tuesdays, it is jazz night,
With Wednesday's Mystic Meg,
I hope I don't fall down the stairs,
And break my bloody leg!
You have to give her credit,
At least where credit's due,
As running a pub as good as this
Must be hard to do.
When it comes the weekend,
A nice good crowd she gets,
And mention fun, with loads of rum,
And Eileen, she says 'Let's!'
Her kids are Helen and Tony,
Nor forgetting Becky the dog,
Who always hides behind the chair,
When I bring down young sod.
She is a real nice person, as anyone can see,
And when I've run down on my luck,
She's always there for me.
Don't think that she's a pushover,
And please don't take the mick,
As liars, cheats and spongers,
Well they just make her sick.
I'm going to end this poem,
As I've finished for today,
And if you want a night of fun,
Go the Anchor, what more can I say?

Mandy Jayne Moon

CONVERSATION WITH A DEAD MAN!

Racial discrimination was a topic the erudite man
Wanted to tackle with Paddy and find out his view if he can
'There's not such a thing in the graveyard,'
'God love yer honour,' he said
'For bones are all white in the graveyard,
There's equality when you are dead.'

So ended the deep conversation between a live man and a corpse
The bright morning sun was a-rising, the rain falling down in big drops
'I'll have to get back to me kip now,' said Paddy with tinge of regret
''Twas a pleasure to meet you, your honour, I don't want me old bones
to get wet.'

Roy Angus Millar

KEEP FAITH

Things just aren't going your way,
the electric is due, and so is the gas.
The two tall bailiffs continually harass,
knocking on your door from 12 noon daily
always asking the same, 'Are you ready to pay me?'
They cart away your freezer, the table and chairs,
skinning your household bare.
Ever so thorough as they pick through your things,
but alas it's not over until the fat lady sings.
When on the verge of total collapse,
the rent already unpaid.
It's at this time when you sat in silence,
and quietly to your god you prayed.
By some stroke of luck, delivered by fate
four numbers appear on the lotto.
Two hundred pounds to you is on its way.
'Keep faith' is your family motto.

Philip Naylor

HOUSE OF DESPAIR

Welcome to the house of despair
Welcome to agonies' lair
Come hang your senses by the door
Come inside and be my guest

See that guy in the corner
Always blue, forever a mourner
Lived his whole life in misery
Broken and beaten since he was three

See the boy with the broken crown
Watch him cower, cry and frown
Bullied and tortured in his school
Yet he's the one made the fool

See the girl with bruised fists
The red ring around her wrists
No one seems to understand her
Only will in the funeral parlour

See that lady in the red
Saw her family all shot dead
Now she sits all day alone
Yet still waits by the telephone

See the woman who was violated
She should be the one hated
Now too scared to see the sky
Just sits inside, would rather cry

Welcome to the house of despair
Everyone ignores, no one cares
All walk past, get on with lives
As I start passing out the knives.

Adrian Salamon

FALLING STARS

Look into my eyes
Deep inside
Try to find my soul
It's there for the taking
It's yours in the making
Forever and a day behold!

I looked into your eyes
Deep inside
I tried to find your soul
But what I found was breaking
It wasn't mine for the taking
Forever and a day behold!

Closing my eyes
Trying to hide
The pain of your confession
My soul has broken
At the words you have spoken
Forever and a day behold!

Emma Scott

WHERE DID ALL THE INDUSTRY GO?

Chimneys billowed chuffs of smoke,
Drifting skywards to sleep on the town,
Lying on the skyline, smog from the kilns,
Meant to stay and never come down.

A flourishing industry back in the day,
Bottle ovens stood proud and tall.
All manner of wares made and sold,
And now there's nothing at all.

One by one they ceased to live,
Each pot bank ripped from its roots.
Gone forever, just memories left,
And photos existing in books.

Jennifer Austin

NATURE AND ME

A gentle breeze as light as a lover's kiss,
The cardinal warmth of a July evening.
Endless amounts of copy, forge that is so natural.
Falling short constantly as the image lacks the life of its scenery,
Our countless lives echo that around us,
Both beauty and harshness.

We sit and wonder who, why and what made this corner shop of nature.
Whilst openly covering any last elements with man's own grey palette.
The colours of allure are mimicked over constant adverts,
Choice is nothing sought after, compromise seldom sought.
Both primal elements of nature and its love for everything,
We sit and judge nature as if somehow above it.

Ian Fisher

HERE AGAIN

Bonfire Night will be here once more
People are so frightened they keep away from their door
Why do they sell fireworks before Bonfire Night?
People misuse them; they give us such a fright
People get hurt and in hospital they land
Why can't fireworks now be banned?
Yes fireworks are a wonderful sight
But to misuse them they have no right
Organised bonfires are quite good
Selling fireworks to them is what they should
I don't buy them for my kids at all
I want to see them grow up, unhurt and tall
So why instead of profit, start to think of lives
Too many people get hurt and some die
When will they be told
It's no fun anymore?
You may realise when it comes to your door.

Anne Davey

REST ASSURED

A romantic interlude came about, should I go another route?
So many years since we last met, now it seems another test
No longer young, we meet again, in a future that's unforeseen
Health not good, set in our ways, we have known happier days
And in times we both have known, never a moment on our own
A lifetime friendship it has been, ever moving changing scenes
Health a problem for both of us, let's to our health drink a toast
Whatever destiny commands may even be in a foreign land
We drink together, you and I, and talk about the days gone by
Rest assured, it's meant to be, magic moments for you and me
Recalling all our younger days, and the funny jokes you made.

Joan Prentice

A Young Man Dying

The spring of life now ends for me,
My summer, autumn will not be,
For winter comes early, uncalled,
The reaper rides my shadow bold.

My mortal shell is looking great,
A cancer within creeps, I hate,
So quickly life now ebbs away,
My flush of first manhood at bay.

My mother saw my spring flourish,
My summer, autumn now vanish,
I know she cries but never lies,
The sun will set with many sighs.

My years are counted now in days,
I dreamed a soldier brave always,
I raced with horses, crests of waves,
My dreams still dreams, my mind their caves.

I heard the songs of birds in spring,
I did not know my life would swing,
From spring to winter, age no thought,
My leaves are buds, with life I fought.

I hope when mortal shell is shed,
That pain will not visit my deathbed,
I pass asleep to Heaven's gate,
The angel's spring will recreate.

David M Walford

FENLAND LAW

Balaclavas and the law
Hand in hand for sure
Baseball bats rule
If you don't believe me
You're a fool
People not safe at home and work
Because villains do lurk
Defend your home
And see them go free
Harm them in defence
And you're before the bench
Be brave and give evidence
Raise the roof
Only to be told
There's no proof
They laugh at us under masked faces
They are cowards
And think they're hard cases
Maybe we need a secret society formed
Use every dirty trick
So we can keep out of the nick
Revenge the key
Ask no fee
All in a good cause
Without remorse
No quarter given or asked
Dish out justice and unmask
The die is cast
Fight to the last.

Richard Pollington

MORE TO SHARE

A babe laying in a manger,
Things have happened which were stranger,
But we should not leave Him there,
For there is more to share.

A child of twelve in the temple discussing the Word,
The teachers were amazed at what they heard,
But we should not leave Him there,
For there is more to share.

He healed the sick and raised the dead,
Many were touched by what He said,
But we should not leave Him there,
For there is more to share.

Before His accusers He stands,
Soon there will be blood on their hands,
But we should not leave Him there,
For there is more to share.

As on the cross He dies,
The thief unto Him cries and with salvation He replies,
But we should not leave Him there,
For there is more to share.

From the grave He arose,
Appearing to those whom He chose,
But we should not leave Him there,
For there is more to share.

To the Father, He ascended,
My poem is not yet ended,
In our hearts, He should be found there,
With others His Word and love we should share.

Louise Keene

A Poet's Life

It's a tough life, being a poet;
and I feel that others should know it.
Sitting all day, there on our bums,
scratching our poor heads, for words that won't come.

We don't rise 'til late, from out of our beds,
breakfast is brief, as newspapers are read.
'Inspiration', is that which we all seek,
all through the long days, week after week.

A4 paper abounds - in sheets, mountain-high,
whilst dormant - our pens, point up to the sky.
Our shoulder-length hair, goes with the job;
sometimes you wish, for just a short bob!

What might our editors want us to write?
That is the question, that nags day and night.
Should we be topical or historically bent;
say what *we* think, in those items sent?

Then out flashes a pen; inspiration at last,
(sitting just thinking was a pain in the a**e!)
the muse comes upon us; we fervently write,
will this be published, is it alright?

There's no money of course, in forging these words;
I doubt if our names, will ever be heard.
Few are up there, with Wordsworth or Keats,
but then I guess, this won't lose us much sleep!

Peter Mahoney

THE UNFORGETTABLE 11 09 2001

I beheld on TV, that cursed day in history,
The cruellest act in my concrete memory
When a handful of worms in human form
Felled humanity with Hell-jets from the sky.

Unarmed and unsuspecting, unoffending women
And men minding their morning's work-regimen
Became cornered and compressed like *papadams*
And burned like firewood in fountains of flames -

Timeless to telephone homes or husbands or wives.
Some lost their limbs and then their lingering lives;
Some scorched in their seats; some in lifts or stairs
Vying to flee; many in teeth of Twin-Tower rubble.

Scared, shuddering workers screamed; limbs twitched
Without heads; some lost sight; minds got unswitched;
Few shattered like shrapnel while quite a few cooked
Like chunks of meat, roasted, baked. Over 3000 died.

I sat shocked and still for a whole half-hour and five
Witnessing it all, fleeting between Channels 1, 3, and 5
From 2pm abandoning a pre-planned after-lunch nap,
That off-Tuesday; also my meals and everything else.

How did it happen? Why in your Heaven's holy name
Was that massacre ordained, Good Lord? What shame
Those derailed airborne devils were born at all
To maim New York, the US, and the human race!

Kopan Mahadeva

LIFE

The way of life, is it a pattern?
Is what happens meant to happen?
Is there a story which has already been written?
A story which has past, present and future?
Has what we do, already been done?
Has it been done because it was written by some?
Is there a reason for the things we do?
Life is a peculiar thing, this I know is true!
Life is the biggest mystery of all.
It's like we're climbing a great big wall.
Sometimes the wall gets so steep we fall
But sometimes we are given a ladder
And climbing this wall does not seem to matter.
Some people treat life as a game,
Others don't treat it the same.
Each of us deals with life in our own little way,
Whether it's full of worries or play.
Life should be taken day by day.

Katie Davies

WAKEY... WAKEY!

Alarm bells ring out stridently from a million bedside clocks,
Waking workers reluctantly as they prepare to pull on socks,
Crawling sluggishly from the beds, yawning - still half-asleep,
Across the chilly bedroom floor on shuffling feet they creep.

Into the vacant bathroom to shave and wash themselves awake,
They can't afford to miss their train, their livelihood's at stake,
From Monday to Friday every week, hired workers bound they be,
But when Saturday comes, for two whole days, they're liberated - free!

They can picnic in the countryside, perhaps stroll out with a friend,
Maybe even stay at home and have a 'do-it-yourself' weekend
The people may be young men - perhaps middle-aged or even old,
They may be retired veterans, or dashing Romeos brash and bold,

But whether they be happy or sad, whether joyful or forlorn,
To be society's servants, all who work for a living are born,
Day by day they laugh or cry, often driven beyond their capacity,
Ensuring that each and everyone can share in Britain's prosperity,

The majority will receive no medals in the annual Honour's race,
But who among our citizens has greater right to pride of place,
Without the workers' skills and dedication in oft unrewarded toil,
This dear Britain we all cherish would be but beggared soil.

F R Smith

GRAVESTONES

A willing craftsman cut this stone,
With chiselled edge and polished face,
To please a grieving customer
And earn a spartan crust.

In loving memory, inscribe
Who passed away, who died in grace.
To Rest in Peace. In God we trust.
Eternal Life. Forever Blessed.

The widow - she remembers well.
Her man lies deep beneath the script.
He'll not be seen again today,
And soon the grave's unvisited.

The winters come, and go and come.
The orchards die, and sprit, and bloom.
Grieve for those who grieved. And grieve for *them.*
Remember those who did remember their remembered.

But caskets crack and tombstones lean.
Weathered letters brown and green.
The crumbling mark of mason's craft
Is buried too in ivy's raft.

Who sits an hour in graveyard still -
Who sits an hour with time to kill
Will see when notion's set to rhyme
That very stone is killed by time.

David Light

THE PARKS OF OXFORD CITY

On Old Shotover Hill, nobody sleeps,
They all walk their dogs for pleasure,
They solemnly watch, wait and keep
An eye on their pets for their leisure.

Dogs down rabbit holes, rolling in the sand,
Shotover's fun in Oxford's land,
Eating ice cream cornets every single day,
On Shotover Hill, children and animals play.

In Cutteslowe Park everyone plays games,
Football and tennis too,
Running and skipping over the plains,
Oxford's fun for me and you.

On Southfield golf course, adults play,
Where the golf balls fly so high,
Hitting the balls up, up and away,
Some of the balls scraping the sky.

In Southfield Park in the sun,
Everyone from Cowley is having fun,
Some of them have fun at the fair,
Or on the swings up in the air.

There's beauty in Oxford's parks,
With people everywhere.
Children playing and having a lark,
Flying kites high up in the air.

The Warrior Poet - Eamon John Healy

HALF TERM

School holidays here at last! Hip hip hip hooray!
Enjoy the summer break, but also be safe, we say,
Slap on the sun cream, wear a hat out in the sun
So you won't get burnt, as it will spoil your fun,
Do always tell your parents where you will be,
So they won't be worried if you're late for tea.

Never talk to strangers, especially if in a car,
No matter how friendly, it may seem they are,
Remember 'look both ways' before you cross a road,
You must always practise the 'Green Cross Code',
The 'churchyard' isn't a playground, there are parks,
It isn't 'cool' to vandalise or write rude remarks!

Water is an attraction, usually safe if there's a lifeguard,
But learn to swim in the baths not where it is barred,
Building sites and railways are dangerous places too,
We're not having a moan but just thinking of you!
So all of these warning, please try hard to remember,
Helping to keep you safe until back at school in September.

G Siddall

COMFORTABLY BROKE!

From pen to paper, from mind to ink
The words I write are the words I think
Simple at first, later much more clever
As wise as the owl, as unpredictable as the weather

Diabolical and directive are the things I think
The pain, the horror, the panther in pink
Cartoonist in a way, narrow-minded of course
Expected to be like a robotic-trained animal
For example a horse.

So what way could I get out of this vertical hole?
Upwards obviously but it won't be a stroll
It's dark down here and the light's far from close
And before I can focus, the door slams on my toes

Because you see life as it stands is tough, cruel and sweet
You pass through hard times before you land on your feet
And as I write this here nonsense in the hope of fate
Or a break from this reality that drowns me in hate

I keep on searching, hoping for wealthy peace of mind
But then life once again can be so unkind
Twisting and dragging me down demanding respect
From me disrespectful in retrospect

Insanely sane, childishly mature
From the peak of a mountain to the depths of the ocean floor
I start where I began and end up where I was before
My hunger to be comfy could satisfy my thirst
The latter as in this poem irrelevant to the first . . .

Matt Riley

SLEEP

As I walk into the shadows, I see my place is not out there,
As I stay in the darkness; can I hide my past deep secrets?
Forgotten images press their heavy smoke against my delimitation,
My mind is racing to hide from this emerging cost I am feeling;
When I look out and see the world of lies, I feel unaided - forgotten.

I was only a boy and could not hope to be rescued from my pain,
The walls were too strongly upheld and the fortress was impregnable,
The guards were from my own kin and were looking the other way,
But always with one eye keeping me in check - to be the good victim.
Life dealt me a vacuum of uncertainty - a hole to get lost into.

The shadows feel less protective as I move to understanding the cost,
Something is rising from within - like an inflorescence to be viewed
                                                                    in awe!
Something that moves from within; like a liquid sliding out of a
                                                                   glass vessel,
Pouring out to be witnessed by the world of blinkers - the world
                                                                   of danger.
The cost of life is to be a pretender and dance the danger with
                                                                fancy footwork,
But my dance is slowing down and is resting on my own shoulders
                                                                'to sleep in peace'.

Ricky N Lock

RAGS TO RICHES

I tried so hard to make the grade,
So tidy, clean and smart.
It only served to cover up
Such pain within my heart.

I trudged the high street, chose new styles,
Attempted to look cool.
The credit card just mounted up,
I'd been had for a fool.

I so much wanted to be loved,
Approved, liked and admired.
Somehow the fashion gems were dross,
They all seemed plain and tired.

But wait, it spoke about my plight.
The Bible was so clear,
And all the goodness I'd achieved,
The things that cost me dear

Were classed as 'filthy rags' you see!
A great big ugly mound!
And, like the son who'd fed the pigs,
The smell still clung around.

Then Jesus said, 'For you I died,
It was My life I gave,
And now, don't strive and struggle so
Like some poor wretched slave.'

I've left the world of trashy glitz,
And tawdry-labelled gear,
Jesus clothes me in holiness.
The path ahead looks clear.

Forgiven, washed and cleansed and dressed,
In brand new robes of white.
A princess, clothed in righteousness,
And precious in His sight.

Gillian Humphries

THE DOG

(Keep away from china dog)

'Hi, I'm a dog, my name is Bob,
I'm a family pet and that's not a bad job,
When I first came here I was nearly new,
My mum didn't mind me going as she had quite a few,
I like it here with these strange human kind,
They feed me well and take me out,
Sometimes I think they can read my mind,
To prove they love me they even save my crap,
In a little bag and take it home, now that is strange I find,
My dinners are always put on the floor,
In case the bell rings, so I can fly to the door,
I sleep in the kitchen, perhaps it's because I snore,
My ears are always alert even when I sleep,
To protect my family and home from someone on the creep,
When someone I don't know comes along,
I bark and growl; my folks say, 'Shut up, lay down!'
Sometimes I don't know if I'm doing right or wrong,
As when the strangers have gone away,
They say, 'Good boy' and pat me on the crown,
But they are the crazy humans, I'm just an old dog, OK?

Roy Kimpton

Remembrance

We walk this land
Where battles raged
Beneath the earth
Lay men not aged.

They sacrificed
For us to be
What we are
And what we see.

They gave their lives
Their limbs, their sight
Peaceful men
Who went to fight.

If we forget
It is our crime
They gave their all
For us, this time.

Suzanne Thorne

Dawn

Elusive sleep
Nightmares creep
Wake me awake
Until daybreak

Photos images
False premises
Given wide range
Accept, change
Rampage thoughts and past
Old ghosts, aghast.

Sheila Cheesman

WINTER'S WOE

Winter's cast its icy stare,
O'er the fields and tree so bare,
While country creatures hibernate,
Dormant deep in oblivious state.

The sky is black and full of snow,
Disconsolate cattle seem to know,
By trampling o'er the hardened ground,
That food for them has to be found.

The days are now not very long,
And sad to say the sun's not strong,
And darkness couples with the cold
To lend its might to winter's hold.

Eddie Main

IT SEEMS

It seems I'm not much good at 'stuff'
Would I do better as a poet?
And if I never try it out
Of course I'll never know it
The effort I put into things
Is not enough - it seems -
So me - as a poetic bard -
Is beyond my wildest dreams.
It seems - I don't have confidence
To bring these words to light,
For yet again - it seems to me -
I just won't get it right!

Eileen Stuart

REMEMBER THEM AT CHRISTMAS

At Christmas time we're all too busy
getting in the party mood,
unwrapping presents and drinking wine
and eating too much food.

Christmas time is somewhat hard
especially in poor countries abroad,
for giving gifts to the ones they love
are luxuries they just can't afford.

Remember them this Christmas time
when that turkey you start to carve,
there are people who cannot afford to eat,
those poor people, they will starve.

If I could ask for one more wish
I'd say to God above,
'Please take care of the needy this year
and send them our thoughts and our love.'

Rachel Ford

ON THE DEATH OF A SEAFARING BROTHER

He sails the seas . . . captain of his own ship,
confidently moving towards that final port of call,
knowing the terrain from tales long told,
and visualising the map, which over the years
has become as familiar as his own self.
His destination is known to him,
he will arrive amidst jubilation,
and music will announce his coming!

Jean-Angela Smith

BEING A KNEE

Sometimes I'm covered
Other times I'm bare
I'm located in the middle of the leg
Yes, that's right, the bend down there
Every day I'm relied on, to get the body around
When I was younger I was abused . . .
A fall in the playground
I'm the one that got bruised.
But now I'm older, you could say wiser
Because when the body sits at a table I duck
In many years to come I'll be older
Frail in my later days
After my support for the body, who's going to support me?
Am I to retire after years of loyal service?
So when you're walking around, please think of your knee!
I'll always be a good friend from the day you're born until you're 83!

Emma Scott

DALLAS

November '63, seemed like eternity
Attending Holy Trinity elementary
Nuns took us for a stroll
Down Oak Lawn, to be a part
Of history's show

Saw Ruby's purple-cushioned bar
Giving kids candy made him a star
It was a flash as we stood still
A wave, a smile, a little boy's thrill
I moved away after that day
Never recovered, never stayed.

James Patrick Milton

A Truthful Hanging

What man of opinion or honesty fair
Takes time at a hanging to stand there and stare.

Which judgement is his to throw that first stone
To clench o' the fist to break that bare bone.

For the good and so righteous, grieve a dignity's cause
When moral men, mocking men, make morality's laws.

Where man would veil vanity with such slyest o' smile
Deception's deceit would tread many treacherous mile.

For what sadder sight could man ever see
Than hear bloodlust baying that name honesty.

Moonlight's mirage, casts ne'er a long shadow
Gives gallows fain creak with corpses so callow.

Whilst those whispering widdies would sway in that wind
Reality's death tells o' truths they may ne'er rescind

Where the righteous would talk, their voice very low
That if Devil durst hear them, their false face he'd know.

For man evermore in the markings of time
Heeds no greater sermon such hangings begrime.

And shudders himself if he gives care a thought
What justice be God's when man's truth may be bought.

For there in that light of the moon's fallow beam
Men will in truth's word, their own gods so blaspheme.

Shaw o' Inchrory

BIRDSONG

'Here it comes - Good God - it's passed!'
It had all - that greatness asked
An angel with extended wings
'Farewell dear bird,' a nation sings
We thought forever it would soar on high
But on this day - we must say 'Goodbye.'
What greater loss could befall we
On this sad day - two thousand and three?
For all a pride - that did exist
In future years to be sadly missed
A fatal act brought it to Earth
But honest men brought about rebirth
With swivelled nose - with head on high
Throughout this world like arrow did fly
In skies above - it showed its might
In humdrum days and in still of night
O'er lands afar it did once zoom
To leave in wake - its sonic boom
And thought for aeons it would succeed
Alas for years, some hearts will bleed
But alas the funds were short of 'gold'
Once a joy for all to behold
A bird on wing in Heaven's air
But now regrets - it is no longer there
A 'might' a 'sight' for young and old
The dream that lived! The wonderful *Concorde!*

Jon El Wright

FRIENDSHIP
(To Lesley)

Friendship is something we cannot buy
If we are very lucky
We will have a friend somehow
I have been blessed to have a friend who cares
Who is there for me always, when no one else has cared
We have laughed and cried together
And helped each other through
The hurt and pain that life throws up
The rain has come down on both of us
But we are always there for each other
There's a rainbow in the sky, and I know why
Because my friend and I will be together
No matter what the weather.

Carol Hanney

FREEDOM

I know you look
For tomorrow
And it fills your heart
With sorrow
You won't see
The way I am

So look and believe
For like a field
Lying fallow

It's too hard
For you to swallow

It's true
I wasn't born to follow.

Mick Vick

Dust Upon The Winds Of Time

Dust and shadow, future certain, scant reward for three score years
and ten.
Maybe more or maybe less, who cares, who counts the years of men?
Fleeting shadows are memories of the past,
With time they fade, they cannot last.
And all we are is future dust,
When we are gone, as go we must.
We are dust upon the winds of time,
Distant shadows locked in silent mime.
Dust and shadow, future certain,
The final act, the final curtain.

Vladimir Nikolai Vetchinsky

January Sales

Relish the invigorating,
Deeply intense situation.
Feel the vibes of excitement
Tingle in anticipation.

The manic race begins,
Serge forward be anon,
Gallantly battle through
Relentlessly on and on.

Awaken your confidence,
Face your fear and be brave,
Haggle persistently over the
Infuriating babble of the raid.

Triumphant, revel in the glory
And stand proud,
Gloat over the ever-increasing
Neurotic crowd.

Jacqueline O'nions

TOMBSTONES IN BOTTESFORD CHURCHYARD

They lean like drunken soldiers, in faded dappled grey
Born in some mason's workshop of feldspar quartz and clay
They've weathered storm and tempest, reflected moon and sun.
Telling their dismal story, announcing every one,
the end of some cherished life.

Diverse of shape and outline, these figures chipped and worn
Were made to stand together with purpose uniform,
But some have fallen over and others broken down
having lost their orders, thus failing in their aim
to tell of some cherished life.

*'Sacred to Ellen Catherine,' 'In memory of Anne who died,'
'For Olivia, daughter of Olive and Thomas,'* how they tried
to keep their charges living within the minds of those
wandering this necropolis seeking some repose
reading of cherished lives.

One tells of Thomas dying in seventeen twenty-two
That is the total story, the best his scribe could do.
But Harriet who went later, *'The treasured wife of John.'*
has listed in her orders, *'Father thy kingdom come.'*
bringing this cherished life?

Epitaphs shaped by poets, tributes written in rhyme
using the craft of the wordsmith to freeze a moment of time,
so John Jackson always *'kept his word as far as mortal could
To grieve for him would be absurd,'* because his life was good.
A perfect cherished life?

Some have guardian angels, to watch them day and night,
Still they are chipped and broken finding no respite
From the ravages of time and the planet's constant roll
Their faith in cherubim wasted, if this were point of it all
To preserve cherished lives.

They lean like drunken soldiers, just clinging to their task,
decaying with their charges, their best years long since past
Their splendour now diminished, by wind and sun and rain
Their origins forgotten, buried by passing time
With those cherished lives.

Fulfilling still a purpose, these lumps of rock and stone,
Remind each generation, in life one thing alone
remains, not fame nor failure, nor faith which some things move
but what is left at the very end is the love
Of cherished lives.

Ray Smart

CHARITY SHOPS

I like to browse in charity shops
there are lots of cheap items on sale.
From records and toys, china and books
to clothes hung up on the rail.
By looking through all the stock
(it changes from day to day);
I find just what I am looking for
at a reasonable price to pay.
It's nice to think that the money spent
is going to a good cause,
helping to pay for cancer research
or a cat with poorly paws.
I come away feeling happy
contented with what's in my bag:
for when I buy in a charity shop
shopping is not such a drag.

Mary Hill

LINKS
(Written for British Sausage Appreciation Week)

Time machine take-off! Whiz back through age on age
Till you reach Ancient Sumeria.
Control your rising hysteria.
What do you see? Sumer folk eating *sausage!*
Who gave them this civilising recipe?
Was it astronauts from outer space
Who met the Sumer folk face to face?
'Hi! We bring a cosmic speciality
Earthlings! Pick up dropped jaws and unbulge your eyes
Come! Who'll be the first to take a bite?
Mmm! - Sometimes its skin is rather tight
But you'll find the inside a tasty surprise.

A mixture to boost muscle and brainpower.
A treat your children will not forget.
A meal you adults will not regret.
Soon - you'll build a city called - ahem! - Er - *Ur!*

Your gods and priests alike will enjoy sausage . . .
We note your landscape is rather flat -
So why don't you build a ziggurat?
A sausage feast you enemies will enrage . . . '

No need to linger. Whiz back to present time.
Those primitive sausages just seen
Have served to make you even more keen
To pop some on to sizzle for dinner time.

All sausages devolved for five thousand years
Are *links* between us and early men.
For bangers and mash we cry 'Amen!'
Who knows? Perhaps out there, some cosmonaut hears . . .

It may be the one who turned those Sumers
Into this world's first sausage consumers.

Chris Creedon

THE FLOWER AND THE FIREWORK

Flower and Firework started a race
Firework said 'I speed with great haste'
Flower said 'I grow gracefully in this place.'
But Firework did not listen and into the air it did fly
Flower said 'Stop going fast you will surely die!'
But too late, Firework went higher and higher into the sky
And seconds later, with a mighty bang
Turned dark to light throughout the land
With its splendid lights which lit up the evening dew
Colours red, yellow, pink, white and blue
Then slowly disappearing, leaving forever
Nothing left, nothing to remember.
Flower said, 'Wait, watch patiently for a long time,
I give pleasure just right
With the same effect of that firework with colours bright
Petals open revealing colours red, yellow, pink, green and white
That will last from early morning till end of the night
And when in weeks I start to fade away
I send out seeds of new, nature's way
And keep on giving people pleasure and love
Joy I bring on a wing of a dove.'
So it's not being faster that does matter
Take your time, don't be a mad hatter
So everyone, everything, everywhere
Take your time and take care.

P Brewer

CAROL ANN

You think she will pal,
But she won't.
You think you know Carol Ann mate,
But you don't.

You don't know Carol Ann,
You never will.
Only Carol Ann knows Carol Ann,
And she's a secretive pill,
A combination of explosive chemicals,
Sugar-coated,
Makes her easier to swallow.
Carol Ann is deep,
Her brain's not hollow.
It's full of thoughts,
Full of pride,
She's a lone star,
Not an easy ride.
She's a silent sound,
On her bumpy ground.

You think she will pal,
But she won't.
You think you know Carol Ann mate,
But you don't.

She's not for sale,
She's not for rent.
She can't be taken,
She's never lent.
She can't be coerced,
For a fee.
Carol Ann,
Would not agree.
All this you won't see,
It just can't be.

She's on the moon,
She's lost at sea.
She's in songs,
And books of poetry.
But you won't know Carol Ann,
How could you?
If Carol Ann,
Doesn't want you to.
There is no key,
No right of way.
No public entry,
And she does say,

Carol Ann's on a merry-go-round,
Carol Ann just can't be found.

You think you will pal,
But you won't.
You think you know Carol Ann mate,
But you don't.
You just don't.

Carol Ann Darling

?

Well, if you yearn,
Just to learn,
Then try and figure this.
There's something that's a-missing here
D'ya wonder what it is?
It fits in here,
But not in there.
If it's not clear,
Then you just stare.

D Roberts

EEH! BY GUM!

The human body takes
the strain
of the human flesh
which takes the pain -
wrought from the
weakness of mankind
we tread this life
until we find -

without reasonable doubt
mankind's disgrace
is self-inflicted
throughout annuls of time -
but nothing more hellish
than an extracted tooth
which leaves a trail
of gummy pain -

Like Jaws in films
on the rampage bent,
he needs his fill
and is not content -
till his teeth
have ravished the human flesh -

Did his jaws ache too?
I must confess -

that the advent of teeth
is very cutting -
and any extractions
are most off-putting -
for to be left with falsies
what do we gain? -
Seems life is filled
with gummy pain!

Mary Skelton

Mystery Man

I am the man - the mystery man
Who for many, many years and years
Had charming letters from a Tom Champagne,
Saying that I am the faithful sort
Alas not witty or handsome at all,
But a most reliable kind of chap
One of the chosen and fortunate few
Hand-picked from this area. Really? Me?
From hundreds of unfortunates who
Do not qualify to receive the bounty,
Thousands and thousands of pounds that are due.

When I lie dead upon the hall floor
No one will care much, no one will know.
Then clutched to my bosom, they'll realise
That at last I have won a 'Digest prize'!

Sheila Benard

My Walk

I love my walk around the Mount each day,
In springtime I watch the lambs at play,
In autumn the trees look lovely, with leaves brown and gold,
In winter the scenery is beautiful but cold.

I go to see Fury, a lovely white horse,
I stroke him and pat him, he loves it of course,
He is now twenty-seven years old
And he wears a green coat to keep out the cold.

I take some food and feed the birds.
The greedy starlings are always there first,
Then back home I make my way
And I feel I have done my good deed for the day!

May Ward

UNHOLY SPIRIT

Look! Lichgate's empty shadow
- A brighter band of grass -
'Midst headstone grey and shadow black,
As full moon makes its pass.

Brief journey from that lichgate
- To lay beneath that sod -
Got lost in centuries of time.
He ne'er did meet his God.

For all his life from boy to man,
It was his Sunday place,
To sit and hear and stand and sing,
And learn about God's grace.

But when the graveyard beckoned,
When he was very old,
He did not want to leave his seat
- Nor do what he was told.

He could not help the dying bit
- It was the thing to do -
But as for going up or down
Nor Heaven nor Hell he knew.

'If I have been here all these years
As thundered sermons roared,
Then why not stay and hear some more?
In Heaven I may get bored.'

His coffin went into the ground
- The headstone all did buy -
But none did see how quick was he,
How quick and very spry.

For he soon - with soul intact -
Escaped that wooden box,
And went back in the church to sit,
Through doors - keys turned in locks.

Now still in deathly silence
- No Earthly voice nor choir -
He sits immobile, so intense,
No words to life inspire.

Words had boomed forth those years ago,
The organ swamped that space.
To Heaven he did not want to go,
And Hell? - Why! Such disgrace.

Not Heaven, not Hell, then here on Earth
Is where he would remain.
Of companions there would be a dearth -
Who came, he made insane.

Douglas Bryan Kennett

FROM GREECE TO ENGLAND

I left England when it was raining,
For a holiday in the sun,
I was hoping to find romance,
Meet new friends and have some fun,

This Greek island is so beautiful,
Picturesque and very green,
I sit by the pool read my book,
Feeling calm and quite serene.

By the end of the week I'm feeling well,
Rested and ready to face,
England's weather, the snow and the rain,
My wondrous birthplace.

Joyce Gee

THE FLU JAB

I must go down to the doc's today
    to the clinic now winter is nigh
To receive the injection I have every year
    for the flu from which many folk die

He rolls up your sleeve preparing your arm
    to use the needle which he has now filled
He plunges it in and you don't feel a thing
    and your fears of the winter are killed

You'll never be bothered with winter's cold chill
    with the coughing and sneezing it brings
You can weather the storms and icy-cold days
    which is a wonderful magical thing.

It has saved many a life of those who are old
    as the weather each winter was feared
Now they can bless those medical men
    for their job is now well revered.

Germs are caused through a cough or a sneeze
    and if you don't have the jab for the flu
You may be a victim because of your lapse
    so it's a fortnight in bed now for you!

Lachlan Taylor

My Message

My message I send to you today
On the wings of a pure white dove
For you have shown how much you care
And given to me your precious love.

You've been there when I needed you
And repaired my broken heart
I would like to walk with you
In my life you are a part.

You are a rare and precious soul
That radiates light from within
You took away my saddened face
And replaced it with a grin.

How much you really mean to me
Only those in Heaven know
But as we progress through life
My love for you will show.

Together we will walk hand in hand
With love to lighten our way
I pledge my heart to you my love
'Tis my message a dove brings today.

C S Cyster

WHO AM I?

A year ago I did not know who I was.
I defined myself by the people around me.
I let them tell me what to do and I allowed them to control my mind
Not intentionally.
Where do I fit into all this?
No self-esteem, I didn't love myself either.
I thought more of others than I did of me.
Not that there is anything wrong with that.
I hate to upset anyone
But they upset me sometimes.
Not because they are being horrible
They are just being themselves.
I used to isolate myself,
My loneliness was my shield.
I am beginning to understand who I am
I am loving myself again.
People will always upset me
That is life
I let go of regrets and doubts.
I must not allow fear and intimidation to hold me back.
I need me, I don't need power.
I just need to know who I am.

O A Oshinbolu

TO STEP OUTSIDE

Why is it so hard for me to step outside
When all I can do is to stay and hide?
Why do I feel so scared, so alone,
To step outside my familiar zone?
I want to get out and be me,
To walk out alone, and be free.
Why do I feel breathless, unable to continue?
I envy those that can, like you.
I feel trapped here on my own,
Feeling depressed, feeling down.
I can do it, I really can, with you,
But the way I feel inside, you haven't a clue.
My inner self wants to do everything,
Walking, riding and yes, even flying.
I'd gladly pop a pill or have an op,
If it meant that I could cope.
I want to live life and not feel this way,
To cherish the life, every day.
It's no good your saying, 'You can do it!'
Don't you think by now I'd have done it?
It's no good saying, 'Pull yourself together'
All it does is bring me to the end of my tether.
I need answers, I need help,
To tackle this that I've been dealt.
Don't turn away, don't run,
All I want is to have lots of fun . . .
                       . . . with you!

Linda Chapman

A Tiny Step Towards Tomorrow

I'll take a tiny step forward into a new day.
I have let go of my past, flushed it all away.
You do not see me as I used to be.
Happy-go-lucky, able to walk, be completely free.
Trapped by these wheels, is how I am now
Unable to stand or take a bow.
I pray that one day I will walk once more.
Be able to stand and open a door.
Climb stairs instead of taking the lift.
No longer having to feel my life is a gift.
Do not pity me I have a life of my own.
A disabled car, and fitted-out home.
But how I wish I could use my legs once more.
Go swimming, walking and stop being a bore.
I'll take a tiny step forward into a new day.
I will never let this disability get in my way.
I can do things that others can do.
It's just a lot easier, less of a struggle for you.
It was an accident that took my legs from me
But I will always be totally free.

Jo Lodge

Death Of A Princess

Sleep peacefully, Princess, you've had your time
I would have gladly given mine
To spare so many all their tears
To keep you here for many years
A touch, a smile, you gave so much
To those who suffered, a tender touch
So lay our angel in sweet repose
You'll always be our English rose!

Teresa Kilcullen-Davies

With You

I was not just a body.
I was also spirit.
The spirit within me
gave you warmth and love.
My love still touches you,
as yours touches me.
My spirit will always be.
Now it is free
and is all around
those I love.
Feel my warmth
around you.
Feel my love
within you
and your love
will touch me too.

Sue Tobin

Flowers In Bloom

Lightly-scented pink flower
Exudes an evocative fragrance
It drifts on the air in silence
After a sudden April shower.
It deserves a diploma
For that Heavenly aroma
That invades our senses
Breaks down our defences.
A bowl of hyacinths in a room
Delicately perfumed in bloom.

Rosemary Davies

MY GRANDMA

When I was little we'd come and visit, in your garden I'd play
The grass towered up above my head, the sun shone every day

You'd sit and watch TV, my mum would make you a brew
I'd join you by the table and you looked on as I drew

Six children you had lovingly raised, my mother being number four
Twins then came along, when you thought there'd be no more!

You'd always wear your apron, with your lipstick tucked inside
Even though you were getting older, you never lost your pride

There was always a dish of mints for our little fingers to take
And my mother would remind me of the apple pies you'd bake

The winter came and the days grew dark, you left on a January day
Mother said the angels had come and with them you'd gone away

To a brighter place where the sun always shines and the grass
                                                              is green and long
Where as you walk with the skies above, you hear the angels
                                                              sing their songs

And now I know you're not alone, so when the time is right
I'll sit on the grass once more by your side and hug you with
                                                                 all my might.

Jil Moorehead

BLUE ANGELS

Through this universal force
Angels our soul and body seal
Through our vortex chakras
The revolving energy wheel.

The heavenly blue angels
That guide us from above
Send through Earthly energies.
Unconditional rays of love.

Their divine visitations
Veil cascades of blue
Of ultramarine cobalt Prussian
A plethora of shades of hue.

Realms enter through meditation
It's then we feel them near
To purify our auras
And make them crystal-clear.

On this enlightenment journey
They invoke the healing powers
Around us needful mortals
Positive peaceful showers.

From them we have no secrets
They know us inside and out.
Embody spiritual wholeness
With loyalty and love devout.

Seraphims and Cherubims
Archangels draped in blue
In all our of karns
We know that you'll be true.

Patricia Carter

LIAR'S BUILDING
(Full of gleaming faces)

I sit in a room with lighted faces
Glowing screens of lies and smiles

I sit outside on the hidden grass
Choking so hard on the fallen leaves

I sit alone in a world of hate
The mortars of hate
My only friend

I bury the religious
And plant them all a tree
I bury the wanderers
In nothing but a word

And then I take myself far out
Wailing against the road
Moving fast then moving slow
Jumping high for a liar's tongue

Singing and whistling
Against a broken jaw

Crying and laughing
Against a broken life.

Oliver Pickerin

THE STILLBIRTH

Your little hands
Were as tiny as leaves
Your beautiful eyes
That I haven't seen
Your little feet
Were as cold as ice
To hear you laugh, to see you cry
All of it would've been nice
Your little body
As warm and tender as silk
Just the right colour of sour milk
So we're here to say
Farewell my love
And may you watch over us
In the stars above
May you rest in peace
For your soul to find
You will always be here
In our thoughts, and in our minds
So rest in peace, *our child*
May your soul and spirit run wild
See you soon in the heavens above
You will always have our tender loving *love!*

Anna Yates

A Family Lost In Time

I was never a foolish wisher
But to be like Great Great Grandfather Fisher
In my heart it burns like a fire
And old Augustine was a bonnet dyer.
If you had lived in Old Islington
You would have brought mineral water by Lidington.
Great Great Grandfather Thomas was his name
Making his great mineral water was his game.

I see that Great Great Grandfather Clare
His pictures on tables you'll find there
All day he worked without a single stop
Them pictures on the best table top.
Where the Epping Road did narrow
You found the farm with Great Great Grandfather Farrow.
In them days you couldn't be a skiver
Old John he was a mechanical engine driver.

I always aim right for the top
Like Great Great Grandfather Allsop.
The people he would never bewilder
For old George was a master builder.
If you were around Islington of a night
You may have seen Great Great Grandfather Wright.
To be like James when I was much younger
For he was one of them, a costermonger!

Colin Allsop

THE OLD FIGHTER
(A West London marketplace 1965)

The cheering crowd - the hempen square;
A stammered word, a vacant stare;
The boxing idol - a spot-lit god;
A shuffling gait, a meaningless nod.

The victor's joy - the belt of gold;
A champion crowned - embraced, extolled!
A clear-headed youth, the world to gain,
Had no vision of the ultimate pain.

Men made rich by his strength and skill,
Took no blows when they 'topped the bill':
'Let 'em all come, my fighter's a star' -
Business was done with a flourished cigar.

On his market trestle, with balm to sell,
A posed portrait nestles - awaiting the bell.
He's shown in his prime - a proud fighting stance,
The jostling crowd scarcely gives him a glance.

He's a warrior bold in the ornate gilt frame,
But his deeds have grown cold, no one now knows his name.
A crumpled guitar is a sorrowful thing,
Who can remember the songs it could sing?

Some youths in the marketplace yell 'Seconds out' -
Square up, punch the air, but fear not a clout.
They admire the glamour of TV fight stars,
But have only scorn for the man with the scars.

His balm stays unsold, he stares into space;
It's fifty long years since the crowd knew his face.
Frail he may be, many memories failed,
But some days he recalls the time he was hailed.

Peter Haines

ONE FOR THE ROAD

Waking up. But no one there
One wardrobe standing, with one chair.
Bathroom chores, a brand new day
A single towel, and toothbrush lay.
Breakfast time, a lonely cup
Move slowly, top the kettle up.
One tea bag, bowl with just one spoon,
Another meal, passed all too soon!
Meals for one, not much fun
Perhaps a walk, no longer run.
Don't forget the washing up,
One spoon, one bowl and lonely cup!
Today was different, someone came
Life goes on, a pointless game.
Now settled in my old armchair,
Reflecting, no one here to share!
In truth of course, I'm not alone
Books and music, telephone.
One final drink as night draw nigh,
One bed awaits, time passes by!

T G Bloodworth

AH TO BE YOUNG AGAIN!

Ah, to be young again
To be young again
By sooth!
Ah to be
Young again
And to taste
The fruits
Of youth!

David A Bray

FAME 2003

I sought not this fame, it was thrust upon me
to those who foresaw I'd say, 'Out of your tree!'
In wellies and oilskins sluicing out drains
I was more famous than some wot 'ad brains.
Reality telly was mainly to blame.
Expletives and grime and then more of the same.

With a song and a smile and a *fol de rol fud,*
fame comes to them wot goes knee-deep in crud.

Singers and dancers and poets and such,
beaten 'ands down by me, knee-deep in slutch.
Climbing a ladder to rescue a cat,
or underneath floorboards, removing a rat.
(My ratings, they soared when I cleared out a flat
of a one-time professor whose life had gone splat).

With a song and a smile and a *fol de rol fud.*
we are never so 'appy as when knee-deep in crud.

They sit in their lounges with their TV dinners.
Fans, on their couches, creating us winners.
Bats in the roofs, bugs 'neath their floors.
For such-like as me, they are opening doors.
Three cheers for the fame game, 'Real Bread and Butter'.
At the top of my ladder, 'I start in the gutter'.

With a song and a smile and a *fol de rol fud,*
brass comes to them wot can take all the crud.

There is one new pest though, they say I'll repent
One I've not heard of called a 'Pin-stripe Agent'!
As a Beatle once sang, 'So let it be.'
This problem I'll meet, hequanimitably.

With a *ho fol de rol* and a *fiddle me ree,*
An old-fashioned truth 'Where there's muck there's monee'!

Derek B Hewertson

THE CITIZEN'S CHARTER

We are all equal, these following rights are ours,
No one is superior, or inferior, inequality devours,
Regardless of age, gender, race, colour or religion,
For every single father, mother, daughter and son,
I have the right to ask and need whatever I require,
To express my feelings, good or bad, as I desire,
To refuse any requests or demands I cannot meet,
To have my opinion respected, as others I greet,
To change my mind, maybe, without saying why,
To make mistakes and not be perfect, though I try,
To follow my own values and standards, unaccused,
To say 'No' to anything that violates my values,
I have the right to determine my own priorities,
To not be responsible for others' words or deeds,
To be protected by the law, to be safe, and to know,
When the law is unjust or misapplied, to say so,
To expect honesty from others, as they do from me,
To be angry at those I love, whoever they may be,
I have the absolute right to be uniquely myself,
To feel fear and say so, regardless of wealth,
To say 'I don't know' to anything that I am not sure,
To not give excuses or reasons for my behaviour,
To make the right decisions based on my feelings,
To my own space and time, for personal dealing,
To be playful and frivolous, when I need to be,
To be as healthy, if not more, as those around me,
To be in a non-abusive environment, no one suffers,
To make friends and be comfortable around others,
The right to better myself, to change and grow,
To learn what I need to know, what I could know,
To have my needs and wants to be respected,
To be treated with dignity and respect, as expected.

I have the right, as we all do, to be happy and free,
To be the best parent that I could possibly be,
To raise my children to respect others and the law,
And to keep them safe from harm, for me to adore.

Christopher Higgins

HAPPY AND PITY
(Dedicated to my late friend, Dave Horrocks)

Oh, happy he
And happy she
On whom the reaper creeps
Without alarm.
He does no harm
But, taking one swift blow,
With perfect aim
Frees the eternal spirit
From its weary frame.
For this he came.

But pity he
And pity she
Who, turning, sees the coming
Of the foe.
Parries the blow.
The battle lost, fights on,
Resists in vain,
Then bravely struggles hard
Not to complain,
Bearing the pain.

John Belcher

MY FIRST BIG BIKE

When I espied my big new bike,
I hollered, it was so childlike,
yet I considered myself grown,
well I was thirteen - a milestone!
A huge wide smile upon my face,
my mam and dad I did embrace!

The bike did my eyes bedazzle,
as I jumped upon that saddle!
Dad said I should be careful,
I'd become a wild daredevil,
we lived in a street really steep,
it ended in a sharp left sweep,
catch it wrong and you're a goner,
but I was an ace bicycler!

I travelled miles upon that bike,
once I ended up in a dyke,
when on our way to Hawthorn beach,
and to the main road we did reach,
I skidded hard into a car,
And I was thrown into the air,
I sailed up high, then hit a ditch,
I broke my bike, oh what a b***h!

I was unhurt, just shaken up,
I thought the driver would blow up!
He was concerned that I was hurt,
he saw the scratch, an oath he spurt,
the scratch was huge, he stared at me,
he chased us off aggressively,
I carried the bike four miles home,
but I daren't go in - *fright syndrome!*

Eventually Dad came out,
I thought that I might get a clout,
but all he did was talk it through,
I learned a lesson of value,
the bike repairs I had to pay,
something I recall to this day,
the bike and I had lots of fun,
specially when cycling in the sun!

Alan Adcock

TIME, SPACE

This is time, this is space, together it is what we face.
For space is the place, where time eternally stands,
To sound the chime of passing time,
While the hourglass drips the sands.

The creeping hands, forever fans, the face of the
ticking clock.
Faster, faster, is disaster, slower, slower is sure to lower,
the sound of the loud tick-tock.

To stay in the present, just stand still.
Take a step, and you will, into the future move.
It is also said, to turn your head, your past
you will always prove.

There is notation of the Earth's rotation,
With its spinning gravitational strength,
And is all relative to how deeply we live,
Not a weak measure of length.

When the pendulum swings, the minutes have wings,
And night soon turns into day.
So heed this warning, you may be in mourning
When time steals the hours away.

Dennis L Vasey

TIME CAPSULE

Scotland 2003
Northern part of the United Kingdom.

New Parliament building in construction
To mark the start of Devolution
People not too pleased because
There is no lid on spiralling cost.

Destruction of the World Trade Center
Has put us in a state of fear
These islands have been waiting for
A similar occurrence here.

The world is up in arms against
All forms of terrorism
But sadly we resorted to
Fighting fire with fire.

God's church is splintered into many
Differing fractions
Which are themselves in disarray -
To ordinate or not
Those indulging in perverted actions.

The rise of Islam is with us
Landscape peppered now with mosques
Astronomers have warned of such
A flight of terror from the sky.

My friends, in view of all of this
I doubt if there will be
One living soul left here on Earth
To open this in 3003.

S O S

Opal Innsbruk

GODDESS OF THE MOON

I'll not forget that awesome night
When I beheld the winsome sight
Of she who held the silvered moon
As though a beach ball caught one June!
The vision I observed was rare
And who was I this dream to share?
Yet there she was, as large as life!
Smiling like a new-made wife!
Adorned like Virgin Mary blessed
And by her touch the moon caressed . . .
It was as if she saw its worth,
While we just watched it here on Earth . . .
And merely thought it good as dead,
While she displayed true love instead!
Why should we love the moon at all?
It's hardly worth the time to stall . . .
It just reflects the sun at night . . .
And causes tides to move with might . . .
And gets the poets hooked on love . . .
And yet I'd ask, is that enough?
Who knows if we will colonise?
For now, her beauty filled my eyes
And bid me stop to tell the tale -
As if I were the only male
To wish upon a distant star,
Then praise the Lord or shout 'Hoorah!'
Think of Mary near November!
Mary Christmas in December!
Why should I see a maiden thus?
Reveal such visions or discuss
The Mystic Maiden? Goddess? Friend?
God grant me time . . . to comprehend . . .

Denis Martindale

A Lover's Heart

How do you beat the past,
And will it last,
What do we see,
What will be will be,
What do we know,
What seeds do we sow,
Why be stuck in a mould,
What should we be told,
Who knows who'll stab us in the back,
What's behind our retreating backs?
Where are the gods?
Where are the gods?
What waits in the night,
What remains unseen by our sights,
What image is near,
What do we hold dear,
What is behind closed doors,
Eating at us like sores,
Why change who you are,
Why do we go back to the past?
Why don't we run fast?
Do we view the future with fear,
As it is not near?
If so what now?
What seeds are we to sow?
Where is my treasure now,
Are all my seeds sown?
What is seen through another's eyes?
Why do we not see lies?

How close are we to love?
Will they fly like the doves,
Symbol of truth,
Why do we cry a lake of tears,
What do we fear,
How close are we,
Those who cannot see?
Where do our hearts live?
How many tears do we sieve?
Where do we go as we are all really alone,
Is all set in stone?
What sleeps inside a lover's heart,
What sleeps inside my heart,
Shall I run and look for my love?
My scared little dove.

Shane Quinn

TRUST

You think you know someone
Till they bring you down
There's nothing worse
Than hitting the ground

Finding out they lived a lie
Always asking the question why
Feeling the emptiness and then the hurt
Wishing you could scrape away the dirt

For the rest of my life
I'll carry the scars
Spending my nights, counting stars
I wish I could go back to the start
And carry less pain within my heart.

Maria Jenkinson

I'LL BE THERE FOR YOU

She just couldn't handle it,
There seemed no other way,
Whatever made her do it,
She broke my heart that day.

A phone call full of pain,
The love between two friends,
The hurt within her heart,
Desperation that never ends.

Problems were still waiting
When she awoke next day,
And I felt hurt and angry,
That she'd tried to go away.

When she came home I ran to her,
I had to see my friend,
And when I looked in tear-filled eyes,
I thought my heart would never mend.

I hugged her close and cried with her,
Told her all would be alright,
But that sadness that I saw in her
Haunted me that night.

True friends stay, they stick it out,
When things get really tough
They keep you going in real bad times
Even when they've had enough.

The silence of not speaking
Doesn't mean that I don't care,
A text, a call, when you've needed me,
And I've always been right there.

This poem, I wrote to make you see,
The bond between us two,
And just to say I'll always care,
And . . . 'I'll be there for you!'

Helen Carpenter

THE OLD MINE

The winding wheel is still and stark against the sullen clouds,
It hasn't turned for twenty years, and more,
The slag heap used to smoulder, smell of sulphur, now it's cold,
The wind from off will freeze you to the core.

Old rusty, corrugated roof, that once kept ponies dry,
Flaps noisily each time the wind gusts through,
And lets the rain and snow bleach in to soak the rotting beams,
And fade the painted names the ponies knew.

Across the muddy yard there stands a bath-house, next the shed
Where lamps and helmets hung on numbered pegs -
A cupboard with spare batteries, and pads with leather straps,
To cover miners' knees, and save their legs.

There's pairs of metal, numbered discs, still locked inside their case,
The last thing to be handed to the men,
Before they stepped into the cage, to go down to the face -
These won't be ever handed out again.

Below ground now is silent, but for water drips and rats,
No noise from picks and shovels anymore,
Yet if you listen quietly, you may hear ghostly chat,
From centuries of miners gone before.

Geoffrey Leech

NEW BABY

Our new baby at last has come
It seems a lot of hard work for my mum
Mummy says it's a little boy
And we all think we should call him Roy
Mummy and Daddy love him and I do as well
Be sometimes he does smell.
All Mummy does is change his nappy
I don't know why but it seems to keep her happy
All he does is feeds, sleeps and cries
Sometimes Mummy lets me dry his eyes
But he yells with all his might
During the day and into the night
Mummy said he's too young to play
He just lies about all day
I don't know why he is so small
But Mummy says one day he'll be big and tall
I can't make him play a game
Mummy said at his age I was the same
But I do like my little brother
But I don't think I want another!

Richard Trowbridge

ALLEGORISING LIFE

What do I tell anybody, about this word, allegory?
Two tales within, everybody, all can enter, territory,
clever twist in fateful folly, or dafter be, a silly soddy,
down the hatch to empty toddy, no Lord above, no asking Goddy,
repletion makes me well in body, fill wisdom's cup: so why be sorry?
      Fly to Gustav's Planet Jolly.

C Thornton

AN ILL WIND BLOW THROUGH . . . YOGA!

Mrs Martin, a kindly sort, joined yoga to get rid of her inches.
Astounded by the unfriendliness of her classmates, she carried
on regardless through several scowls and flinches.
Smiling all the while she achieved most of the intricate poses
in a world of her own as they turned away and snubbed noses.
Perhaps they were embarrassed of their obvious spare tyres?
She agreed that they were rather unsightly, she simply closed
her own eyes at night when she donned her winceyette-flowered
nightie.
Mrs M forged full steam ahead as the principal smiled non-stop,
obviously holding Mrs M in high esteem, though she did seem to
laugh a little too much! Perhaps her nature was such.
Was it Mrs M's version of the 'lotus'?
Well at least she did try, unlike most of us!
Later in the locker room, a bustling place, with many a red face,
an anonymous card had been strategically placed for anyone to read -
'Somebody here has farted through this class. Please in future leave the
room for your trapped wind to pass;.
Mrs Martin read and sighed, 'How awful, who might it be?
If it was me, I'd be shamed to death.;
But you see, dear reader, our OPA, Mrs Martin, God bless, is . . .
profoundly . . . stone deaf!

J M Hefti Whitney

TRIBUTE TO MY NEIGHBOURS

Neighbours young, old
Proven friends, mine
Comforters in grief, pain
Father Time, decrees when to leave behind.

Friendship, long to cherish
Ne'er to perish
A friend in need
Is a friend indeed.

Thank you sincerely
One and all
Happiness ensured
Whene'er you rang, called.

Friendship, most precious to me
Gift to treasure
Company given, received
Appreciated, enjoyed, to full measure.

Ivy Lott

GRANDMA'S STORY

I wanted to be famous, to reach the opera stage.
I sang the very latest hits from a very tender age.
I performed at people's parties to rapturous applause.
All of this enthused me and fired me in my cause.
I sang in pubs, I sang in clubs, (I practised in the bath).
I've seen my audience close to tears, but mostly they would laugh.
Yet as the years went rolling by, the vision slowly faded,
Everything, including dreams, was getting pretty jaded.
But tonight I made the centre stage and all my dreams came true.
You fell asleep as I softly sang a lullaby to you.

Carol Ann Awdas

ANOTHER SUNRISE

Another sunrise: Earth awaits,
The countdown has begun.
A spacecraft points towards the stars,
Men's dreams are on the run.

Watchers in their quiet kingdoms,
Far out beyond the sun,
Gaze past the moon onto our world,
To gauge what we have done.

Their starship graced primeval Earth,
And sowed man's seed to tend:
Beneath the ancient skies they planned,
Our birth and final end.

But when and how that end may be,
Only the watchers know,
For man has yet to reach the stars:
His seed elsewhere must grow.

Dave Austin

NO RHYME OR REASON

No reason why the sky is blue,
Or even why I should love you

We met the first time, one winter's day,
And never thought we'd love this way

Our love grew stronger, as the years soon passed,
And we scoffed at those who said 'It won't last.'

Now we are older and wiser too,
Nothing will change my love for you.

Ruth Markinson

GLEE CASTLE

What can be seen apart from my screen
And everything else that's in-between?
Books and paper and boxes galore,
Musical discs, maps and so much more.

On a high shelf I hoard loads of things
That are seldom used, mostly in spring,
Forget all that, there's stuff to explore
Stacked from that shelf right down to the floor.

Science fiction lives in this small room
Where walls brightly painted avoid gloom,
Computer's alive working with me
This is my place, my castle of glee.

Once entombed within its sacred walls
And enthralled by its hypnotic pull,
Here I work alone on whatever,
Slogging away, I'm not that clever.

What do I do when in here alone?
Inside my head my swivel's a throne,
Printer is possum, playing quite dead,
Thence magic flows from things in my head.

Nick Clifton

THE PAST REVISITED

The little lane is still unchanged
As it's been for many years
It's seen its days of happy brides
It's seen its days of tears

The chestnut trees that guard the house
Are golden now and on the ground
The chestnuts crunch beneath our feet
With a rustling popping sound.

Reminding us of children
Who played conkers 'neath the trees
Surrounded by the leaves that fell
And fluttered in the breeze.

The little fields are still the same
As they were in Grandad's day
When scythe upon his shoulder
He went to mow the hay.

The little whitewashed cottage
Is still the same today
And when you step inside the door
The years just roll away.

With Granny's chair beside the fire
You can almost see her there
But her daughter sits where once she sat
She, too, has silver hair.

The little house remains the same
Though a century has passed
And just to look brings memories back
Unspoiled, long may it last.

Isobel Laffin

NATION HOW TRUST?

Costs soaring taxes VAT now on our food
May put CID costs stuffing corruption mood
Antics go shopping puss in fur boots
National Trust must trust, for more votes
Puss state 'Trevor fancy me I knew'
Facts to be published are long overdue
Later postcards love kisses Tenerife
Just once more part not come between
Safe houses in Sandy with tot of brandy
David gannet, money funny help handy

'Cock shot point' not far past Bowness Bay
Video wrens in ivy at dawn in sunray
Little snow on peaks but deserted parks
Now long gone perhaps too late for larks
Cemetery where sleep my only true love
Known 'Arrogant Lady' awaits to meet above
Save homes arranged by the CID key
Condemn steal can't National Trust see
Did not Margaret's mother deliver blow
Why or really cover best if never know

'Protect Mother' excuse, corruption thrive
Your time on my knee was glad to be alive
Knew prosecuting solicitor before came such
Lies in court became so false rotten clutch
One daughter tells others, who to call Dad
As her mother listen so pale, looks only sad
Police stopped me from justice or small house
So you and many could consummate like louse
Have I to pay the price you and Joyce now ask
While National Trust pay you for corruption task

Please Trevor go fast get it into highest court
Your mother, dad, moved my mother I this site bought
Only a few days for wounds did heal over this fine
Exemplary character given at end of time front line
Without your slander or my wife's on your behalf
Hope pack hall give some happiness make laugh
Told three chances to win free this now wonder bed
Come demonstrate like lady with bed not even in red
All know for long time has been no law in this land
Hope with sincerity 'National Trust' trust understand.

John J Flint

IN HIS TIME

'Do not get angry in any way whatever you do'
Says God, who will repay any wrongdoing done to you,
He is eternal, strong, and He's always there
To watch over us in our daily lives and care,
For all our good times in life and also the bad.
So keep going in faith and don't be sad.
Although our problems seem sometimes hard to bear,
We have someone near, with whom we can share,
Our problems in life, so don't get upset or sad,
Lean on God's strength and be so glad.
He is always there when we feel down or blue,
Watching over us waiting to bear our burdens, me and you.
So don't ever get upset, angry or sad
Just turn everything over to God and be glad,
That in His time He'll put all things right,
So don't get angry, instead be calm and polite,
Knowing that in our lives God is in total charge
Of all we say and do, and on that I can't enlarge.

George Reed

NEVER TEST UNCONDITIONAL LOVE

I remember those hurtful words you spoke
A past comparison you made
I thought it was a joke
You should not have tested me
Like you constantly did
From then on you planted seeds
Of doubt into both our minds
Even when I was loving and loyal all the time
For my true love, you chose to be blind
Blinded by anger and rage of your past
Caused us such pain like walking on broken glass.

When you doubt'd those precious words I said
You instantly inflicted past poison into my head.
Even today that cruel blow still remains
Now we're both victims of your past anger and pain

Until one day you'll do it all over again
And remember how it cost you then
You lost me then your lover true
Soul mate and best friend
In time you'll realise your test
Should never have been mine.

It was so destructive, cruel and unkind
Who then was truly blind?

When the present then was only our time
And the past should have been left behind.

Graham Hare

CRADLE SONG

Steve again has got it wrong
This is Rosie's cradle song
'Acacia' does not fill the bill
How could Steve get it on a hill?

The house too small and oh, so bleak
Makes Rose a prisoner so to speak
Ensuite room requires a light
Our Stephen is not very bright.

'We do not need two showers,' says Rose,
'That's only required by such as those
Utility room too narrow too
Steve! You have not got a clue!'

Too much mirrored doors and glass
The kitchenette is just a farce
Dining room much too small
How could our Stephen walk so tall?

'The carpets would not be my choice'
According to Rose's Scottish voice
Steve says, 'Rosie, keep your cool.'
Rose retorts, 'You are a fool.'

'Monstrous garden,' Rosie raved
'Demolish it and get it paved'
Rose now getting quite uptight
Steve says, 'Absolutely right!'

Stephen Forward

THE MOVE

As we bowled along the motorway
High up in the van I sat
I viewed the world with tearful gaze
I was too sad to chat.

I had left my home of 30-odd years
From south to north we went
From lovely Devon I thought was Heaven
To an unknown environment

I saw the soft hills as we journeyed on
And I thought of the friends I had left
And the beautiful view from my window too
And I really felt bereft.

Then the scenery changed as we journeyed on
The views were harsher but grand,
The hills more rugged, the trees more profuse,
It was quite a different land.

I arrived at last at my new home
And then I shed a tear.
There were no hills outside my door -
But some friendly voices near.

Now I've settled in my new abode
And plenty of friends I've made.
With lovely drives in the Yorkshire Dales
And at beautiful places I've stayed

So my move to the north was well worthwhile
And at the doubts I can smile:
I've found another corner of Heaven
It is just as lovely as sunny Devon.

Muriel Johnson

BOOK WEEK ASSEMBLY AT ROBERT PEEL LOWER SCHOOL

On Friday I joined an assembly
To experience the fun of 'Book Week'.
The children were smiling and eager,
All longing to share and to speak.

The teachers had inspired and coached them.
All the classes took turns to recall
Stories and poems they had enjoyed.
We happily listened to all.

The tinies talked all about fishes.
Then a drama of how a young lass
Had exotic fruits slyly stolen
By animals, when she walked past!

3S then skilfully presented
Spike Milligan's poem 'Ning Nang Nong'!
Descriptions of unnamed animals
Were all solved before very long.

The Year 4s made wonderful booklets
Of work based on the story, 'Dear Zoo'.
Their writing and pictures were brilliant.
Perhaps they will become authors too!

Some, obviously disappointed
Because they had no chance to read out
Their own marvellous contributions
Will display their work elsewhere, no doubt.

Doreen Lawrence

NATURE'S GHOST

That sickening smell of cleanliness reached up through my nose.
Why can't it smell of flowers like the aroma of a rose?
White walls, white figures, whispering as they pass me,
I feel like I'm invisible, or drowning in a waterless sea!

A door opens as another closes like wings flapping before my eyes.
I hear the sound of laughter and I hear the sound of cries.
Silence now fills the air accentuating my pounding heartbeat.
I staggered against the wall listening to the sounds of running feet.

As I lay on the polished floor, trying to catch my breath.
I focused on the white figure as it approached like walking death!
It took me to a room, a room so small I felt it crush me.
Its large frame hovered over mine, and I could no longer see.

A bright light flashed in my eyes while its breath covered my face.
Prodding, poking and touching me, it was all over the place.
As the needle jabbed my arm, I tried to open my eyes.
I couldn't move my body but I heard my tormented cries.

A familiar voice reached my ears, it was telling me I'd be okay
Feeling more relaxed; I felt my pain ease away.
To him I'm just another patient, just another case!
When I'm dead and gone, will he even remember my face?

Accepting that I was dying was driving me insane.
Will he remember my torture, or recall my very name?
The beauty of the world and nature was never a love of mine.
But now the smell of a sweet red rose stays with me all the time.

The rustling of the long green grass is a delight to my ears
It soothes my inner feelings and blocks out my fears.
The hum of the bees this summer as they gather up their honey
I hear them like never before, now isn't that funny?

I feel the wind caress me as it softly fondles my hair.
Thinking of all that's living while breathing in the air.
The bird on the branch is singing while the sun shines down on me
I wish I were that little bird living life so wild and free.

These sensations that I'm feeling are just a distant memory
Now that I've passed on to the other side, I no longer feel any!
Why was I ever so blind to the things that matter most?
Each day I wander through nature, now that I'm nature's ghost!

Rose Murdoch

HE

I dream of a lover who is lovelier than anything.
I dream of that lover so engrossed with me he can see no other.
No other lips he wants to kiss, no other voice to hear but mine,
Talking of crazy things, love, lust and no more need to pine.
He respects my knowledge of existence of spirits of those gone before,
He balances me, raises passions in me that no one can compare.
But most of all, I could never kill his passion for me, his love undying,
Near death-defying unfailing sparks for me and me alone.
We feel at one though life's just begun for the two of us,
Day by day it begins again, anew and afresh for each one of us.
We flow together, we fall in together side by side,
No one can stand us apart, or separate our burning to protect each
                                                other's soul.
To live in the knowledge that we are to be one, together for
                            this journey and maybe many more.
His eyes are like a song waiting to be sung that he feels he can
                                            sing in me,
They awaken my core, my essence wanting to play in his.
Unfalteringly he accepts my faults and sees who I try to be,
A better person for all I see, for all I feel, he keeps a flame for me.

Sharon Grimer

SHAKE HANDS WITH BILLY REID

How long before we meet?
Keep the cards face down
Play me one more tune
On the seamy side of town

It's not too late I know
For blood to hit the spot
Rise and fall and up again
Billy, I hope you had it hot

They lit your fire in vain
Did it burn too bright?
I'm going on the seamy side
Along with Billy tonight.

Shake hands with me my son
See what we've missed
How far did you get?
Were you even kissed?

What a time we're having
Or is it another dream?
She's doing something to Billy
That I've never seen!

So we tasted life at last
One of us will sleep too well
Shake hands with Billy Reid
There's nothing more to tell.

John Marshall

REMEMBER SCHOOLMATES

Hey up kid! Here we are reminiscing again,
About time we were at school at Broad Lane,
How, at dinner we used to run down to see t'steam train,
Over a mile in seven minutes, or we'd miss it and go insane.

Rattling under that bridge, eighty miles an hour, could have gone faster,
If it hadn't had to stop eight miles lower down at Doncaster,
Like I said to Bill White and his mate, Barry Ullman,
It's well worth the dash - just to see t'West Riding Pullman.

Kids today don't have the thrills we had going home for dinner,
Running home and back, two miles each way, they'd be a lot thinner,
Mam's dinners were full of natural nourishment,
No wonder we could take a sight more punishment!

Punishment in the form of hard graft is what I refer to in our time,
Cos when we'd finished schooling - most of us went down the mine,
None of them left now though - is there old mate?
So what prospects are there now when you come out of t'school gate?

Can't imagine their trains running at eighty miles an hour, down t'line,
No British steel to guarantee - no buckling, and everything's fine,
Our steam engines weighed about hundred and eighty tons,
And they still hold t'record for t'North Eastern runs.

Now we are nearing eighty and can't run for t'train, like we did,
Thee, Billy and Barry and me and our kid,
But in your absence I'll drink a toast to you all and wish you well,
Here's to me and our lass's husband, not forgetting me sel'!

Jack Edwards

SELECTIVE HEARING

'D'you want a cup of tea, love?'
I ask him. Up speaks Jeff,
'Yes please.' He heard me *that* time
But, most times, he seems deaf!

'You said we'd decorate this room.
Shall we select some paint?'
I check if he is listening.
I thought so - no he ain't!

'I saw my friend this morning,
We had a lovely chat.'
He sits and reads the paper
And idly strokes the cat.

'Did you phone about the mortgage
And see what's in the bank?'
He just watches the telly and
His eyes have gone all blank.

'The children need new shoes next week,'
I mention, feeling glum.
He doesn't answer, yet again.
I might as well be dumb!

'Your mate left you a message.
He's going to watch the fight
Then down the pub straight after.'
He heard me then alright!

'Shall we have an early night then?'
I query. He looks keen.
He's actually listening!
Just shows you what I mean . . .

If you don't say just what they want
To hear, they tune you out.
It's called, 'Selective hearing'.
What *men* have without a doubt!

Anne Gardiner

BRAMBLE BUSH

Love is like a bramble bush,
Strong and very lush,
And its fruits come forward in a rush,
Like a sweet voice singing,
That of thrush,
But beware,
Go further,
And enmesh,
It snags your hair,
And tears your dress,
And leaves you feeling in a mess,
Do not listen to the bramble song,
Saying, 'Pick me, pick me,'
For like love, the bramble has a sharpened prong,
Saying, 'Prick you, prick you!'
And at its onset, out to trick you
Like bramble, love has a sweet fruit,
But its stragglers trip you up en-route,
Now at this verse you might titter,
And say it's just me feeling bitter,
But like love the bramble has many snares,
Encroaching on traveller unawares.

Alan Pow

COMPARING YOU TO THE WEATHER

You are like a ray of sunshine
That rises early too.

Full of energy and bright I can't believe
I'm up with you.

You dance on your bare feet
And the sun beams down on you.

The rain, is not always bad news for you.
Bring in the washing, I'm soaked too.

I'm tired but the sun's here to stay.
I sense you are at play.

The sun likes to rest as you do too
Until tomorrow, you will have lots to do.

I love you more each day, son.

Parveen K Saini

OLD-AGE MISERY

Can you remember, how life used to be
When you were young, and not so 'grumpy'?
A spotty teenager, one of them from Hell
Your black clothes and lipstick, and rock-solid gel
You strutted your stuff, thought you looked great
The kids of today, you complain they're a state
But come on you old git, use that memory charm
Remember the way 'you' were, you caused no real harm
They look over to you, and think 'I'd rather be dead'
You look over to them, with a heart full of dread
So enough of the good old years, the tinted colour rose
Generations of teenagers, all sheep in wolves' clothes!

Mandy Lee

My Little Dog

I have a fat and hungry hog
Although he's just a little dog
With a belly that's so big
He's more like a pot-bellied pig.
The scruffiest thing you ever did see
Always there, tail wagging for me
Even on the wettest of days
He will have his own little way
When he looks at me I will concede
And go to the cupboard to get his lead
A walkie somewhere in the park
At every dog, you know, he'll bark
Cocks his leg at every tree
He really is a sight to see
One bent ear and tooth stuck out
Head cocked sideways, that's no doubt
Fur tousled all over the place
Makes me laugh to see his face
As in a race, he's through the door
Muddy paws all over the floor
So mop and bucket at the ready
I wish that he would take it steady
I never could really explain
But he's got away with it again!

BJ

TRUTH

Have you thought of truth?
It's beyond our understanding of truth
Its value is so great
It has lasting goodness
It's most beautiful to read or hear
Truth is very sacred
When we speak the truth
We honour Him whom is truth
He said, 'I am the way, light and truth'
Keep shining with love and truth
Keep searching with love and truth
Keep searching its purity
Its power is beyond our understanding
It's stronger than anything here below
Truth is not fully valued
Evil tries to kill truth
It can't because it's Holy, thrice Holy

M Lane

IN MY EYES

'Dynamite
Explodes'
In my eyes
No reasons how
No reasons why
Then darkness
I need
And darkness
I feed
When 'dynamite
Explodes'
In my eyes.

P Allen

RETIRED!

Fag hung from lip,
Cup of tea sip,
On doorstep sit,
In morning's sun.

From work retired,
Use expired,
Old bones tired,
To gardening turn.

Flower beds weed,
Compost feed,
On planted seed,
And scarecrow hung.

Yard is swept,
No leaves left,
And rubbish kept,
On bonfire burn.

In stocking feet,
By burning peat,
Newspaper read,
When day is done.

Frances Ridett

NO OXYGEN ROOM

In the room with no oxygen, is a room with no life.
The room with no oxygen is somewhere all the time.
The room is so peaceful not a sound to be heard,
Don't try to go in there because it will be your last word!

Jennifer Edwards

THE WITCHES

A tale to tell that will send a chill
About the three witches of Pendle Hill
A long time ago in 1612
When times were hard and fear did dwell

Three ladies did a coven make
A cauldron used for a life to take
They were asked by another
To rid his wife of her lover

And then on one dark winter's night
Their scheme took place and came alight
Tempted to a secluded site
Elizabeth Southern took his life

Now this tale doesn't end there
The three of them carried the body to their lair
Placed him whole into the pot
Began to stir and didn't stop

His bones they ground up
Till they were dust
To cover their tracks
This was a must.

The price of this the husband wouldn't pay
Blackmail was his only way
He tried with Elizabeth, an affair to begin
But when she refused, he turned them in

So arrested, tried and to the gallows sent
With no time for the three to repent
Hung by the neck till they were dead
So now the entire story has been said.

Leslie Tomlinson

PETER
(Written in commemoration of the 25th anniversary of the Battle of Britain)

Peter was young and brave and true,
A son to be proud of, the son of you, and you,
For there were many Peters among the gallant few
Who fought, and died for us, in those skies of blue.
He was in his late teens and his twenties when he answered the call
To save our dear island. For the sake of the world it must not fall
To the enemy, the malignant growth now spread across Europe,
In a few brave young hands hung the world's last hope.
Peter was young and brave and true,
In Spitfire and Hurricane fighter he flew,
And it was with pride he wore his uniform of blue,
The colour of the mist that hugged our shores while still on the rose
                                              hung the morning dew.
But each day that dawned could be Peter's last,
And sleep, for him, was a luxury that belonged to the past,
The call to, 'Scramble. Scramble,' came by day and by night,
It came in the morning, in the evening and before dawn's early light.
It came whenever the enemy planes were in sight,
And each time it came Peter knew it could be his last flight.
He knew how to live; he knew how to die,
Peter who fought in the pale blue sky.
Last night he joked and laughed with Bill in the Rose and Crown,
This morning in a blaze of flame his plane came down.
Peter was young and brave and true,
He fought, and he died for us, in those skies of blue.

Anita Cooling

THE SILENCE!
(Written two weeks after losing my wife after 52 years of happy marriage)

The silence is the thing
I wait alone, no lovely voice
'What breakfast, darling? That's your choice'
No smile for you, no little kiss
These are the wonderful things I miss
That special glance between our eyes
Those years of love, those special ties
We were two people rolled into one
You were to me my moon, my sun
That light has gone
And where it shone
There is just blackness and despair
The songbird's lilt I cannot hear
I am alone. All on my own
The silence is the thing!

Alan Vann

NINE/ELEVEN

I stood transfixed in disbelief before my TV screen
Shocked and horrified by every hideous new scene
I watched those fated planes tear into the Twin Towers
Saw all the devastation in the following dark hours
I listened to the agony of those who had had been saved
And wept for all the victims whose lives had now been waived
I prayed for all the rescue teams to be kept safe and well
As they searched among the debris of that ghastly living hell
I felt all the grief and outrage that a human heart can hold
The ruthless inhumanity still makes my blood run cold
That cruel and ignominious act ensures we all remember
An infamously, tragic date - the eleventh of September.

Jenny Hitchen

My Terra-Nova

I have written poems, I have made up rhymes,
Said many things, many times,
But I have never really said to you
How grateful I am for the things that you do.
You are always there, come rain, or shine,
I am glad you are a friend of mine.

Your willing hands, your winning ways,
Help me through my darkest days.
You are there for me, many others too,
I bless the day that I met you.

I love and admire you from afar,
To me you are that 'special star',
May God reward you for all the things you do,
As I now thank Him for a friend - like you!

Brenda Nicholson

Ride Your Horse

You ride your horse at midnight
Across the frozen ground
To try and catch the midnight stage, oh yes
For away your lover is bound.

You ride your horse at midnight
After the stage running away in full flight
You are still trying to catch it, oh yes
To make them stand and fight.

You ride your horse at midnight
Yet sometimes can be seen
Alongside the stage, oh yes
On a night so cold and mean.

Keith L Powell

BRITTLEBANK FARM

My time has come to say goodbye
To a place called Brittlebank Farm
Where I would watch the sun rise in the sky
Casting shadows round the barn.

The people there were good to me.
Richard, Dennis, Peter, Lea.
Edna, Ida, Hannah too
With little Thomas on her knee.

I've walked through life and prayed to God
Many times I've asked His pardon
And yet He still gave me a gift
To spend some time in this great garden.

Life is short, the path is hard,
But if you are lucky just like me
Go spend some time on Brittlebank Farm,
Stoke-on-Trent in Lower Leigh.

I made my last walk down the lane
There was no sun, just mist and fog.
I turned around and waved goodbye
To my friend, Dennis, with his dog.

A F Mace

EVENING STAR

I heard the soft sound of my lover's voice,
Calling me from my sweet repose.
He spoke to me of a love so true,
But as time went by, it quickly flew.

I heard the soft sound of my lover's voice,
Calling me from the distant hills.
The valleys that lie between are deep:
Knelt by the stream, I gently weep.

I heard the sound of my lover's voice,
Calling me from my dreamless sleep;
Drifting upon the new-born dawn;
Leaving me with a heart forlorn.

I hear not the sound of my lover's voice;
With longing I gaze at the evening star
And I sorrow, knowing it's time to part,
Yet nothing can stop the ache in my heart.

Hazel Mills

ESSENTIALS

Winter means
Trees are bare.
Frost on ground
And mist in air.
Nights draw in
At half-past three.
Then time
For a coal fire
And crumpets for tea!

Lyn Sandford

MY SPECIAL FRIEND

When I think of the jokes we shared in front of the TV,
The delicious chocolate biscuits and the warming cups of tea.
Your witty tricks and funny tales made you so unique,
Never an unkind word would I hear you speak.
Such a loving person with a gentle golden heart,
You are just so special: I hate when we're apart.
Your clever mind and green fingers, your shed was full of tricks,
You were always in there, fixing anything that would fix.

Your Irish tapes you'd sing along to, driving in your car,
Destinations we would travel to, no matter near or far.
Picnics on the green fields, with the family,
Those outings were so precious: such a memory.
Every time I'm lonely, I talk to you in my head,
And every eve I say 'Goodnight' before I go to bed.
There are so many memories that we shared together,
And they'll stay within my heart from now until forever.

Megan Strong (12)

MOTHER'S DAY

Chocolates are being gobbled up
Flowers are being put in bowls
What is this special day?
Of course, it's mothering Sunday
Getting gifts from loved ones
Loving daughters and loving sons
Cards with lovely things upon
Reminds me of a swimming swan
Tulips, roses, daisies too
What else could I possibly do?
All the things that are new
I bought just for you.

Rebecca Bamford (8)

TEST IN LIFE

Born into this world as a baby, I'm unaware
Of what my purpose in life is, or why I'm here
The strange sounds all around me, all the things I see
All part of the confusion, and what life holds for me.

Lots of kisses and cuddles, loving hugs from Mum and Dad
They give me praise when I am good, but scold me if I'm bad
A full security in home life, from birth till I was four
Then life became a big strange world, that happened outside the door.

I'm taken out with Mum, to a place I'm told is school
I'm left alone, told to be good for that's a golden rule
I'm surrounded by lots of children, but still I'm alone in this place
Feeling sad and lonely, looking for a kind friendly face.

Surrounded by frightened children, not knowing what to do
All wishing as I am, that their mum was here too
I know I haven't been naughty, so why have they sent me away
So many toys around me, I'm too unhappy, I don't want to play

I'm told to put my coat on, a bell rings and frightens me
They're taking me somewhere else now, but stop who do I see?
I'm running so fast I stumble, loving arms save me from a fall
My mum is standing waiting, she hasn't sent me away after all

Mum hugs me and kisses me, she tells me not to cry
I need to know why you left me, please Mum, tell me why
She tells me now I'm a big girl, I must go to school each day
To learn to read and write, and find new friends to play

There's no point in arguing for I know what I must do
Now I know I'm not being punished, it's something all children
                                                          go through
So I'll go to school to learn and do my very best
For school is the first lesson, part one of life's long test.

Reimunda Jones

THE DRUNK

Crumpled trousers, dirty shoes,
His breath is vile. He smells of booze.

Down to the pub for one more beer,
His stomach is queasy. He feels really queer.

Out of the pub, once more he is thrown,
Falls flat on his face, then totters home.

His poor wife is waiting, sick to the teeth,
To see her poor husband crawl home like a thief.

He thinks he can stop at the drop of a hat,
But now he's addicted, it's more serious than that.

One more drink he now demands,
Slumps in a stupor and cuts his hand.

Dragged into bed by the scruff of his neck.
The doctor is called and comes really quick.

All tests are taken. Doctor looks grim.
His liver is poisoned, oh, what a sin!

'I'll give him one month. What more can I say?
For a life that's been squandered in this foolish way!'

Florence M Bullen

THE RIVER LEEN

I sometimes walk by the side of the river
Which meanders through Bulwell, the town where I was born
It is a river with a very proud history
But these days it looks forgotten and forlorn

The river originates in the grounds of Newstead Abbey
At the lake where the poet Byron often went
From there it flows through several villages and townships
Until it finally empties itself into the River Trent

The river is part of our local heritage
In past days it served our township well
In its journey it must have seen so many changes
If it could speak it would have so much to tell

It provided the power to drive several mills
In which many local people were employed
But all this has now been confined to history
And most of the mills have been destroyed

At most times the river floats by unnoticed
But sometimes it puts on a bit of a show
At times when the snowfalls have been heavy
The melting snows have caused it to overflow

The river was also a place of entertainment
Where children could fish or paddle for an hour or two
Very few children are seen down there today
Perhaps they have got more interesting things to do.

The River Leen still flows through the town centre
But few people seem to know that it is there
Maybe it's because they are too busy to remember
Or, perhaps it's because they don't really care.

R Martin

RELIEF

The field at first sight is a mess,
Broken guns and cannons are left scattered.
Walk further along and you will see
Just what is in this field with me.

Things that were once human men,
Now their bodies lie in such disarray
Limbs are missing, sight forever gone.
Spectacles of horror, they cause such dismay.

I'm not done in this field of mine,
Many thousands are here, boy and man
We chose to fight in this bloody war,
I wish I could say, 'Stop, no more!'

I will lie forgotten in this patch of land
The war will have ended, life will be grand.
Parties will be given to greet the heroes.
Don't fight anymore. Be friends not foes.

Helen Trevatt

MATELOTS

Oh, Dear Lord above,
Send down a dove,
With wings as sharp as razors,
To cut them their throats
Of them their blokes,
Who sell bad beer to *sailors!*

Andrew Vaughan

An Old-Fashioned Christmas

No more blackboard or sitting up straight
In school dinners please clean your plate
Looking out, chimneys throwing black smoke as they reek
Weather dull, heavy with snow, makes it feel cold and bleak.

Off to the Christmas Service we all go
The teacher puts us in lines of two
Reaching the church door, standing in rows
Waiting to be led to our pew.

The Christmas prayers said
The lesson well read
The chattering and whispers stopped with a glare
Fed up with it all we give our teacher a stare.

We're dismissed and through the door we ran
Down the church steps as fast as we can
Crossing back to the school we are no fool
On holiday, no books - no rule.

Christmas Eve, seeing the magical face of my sister, Holly
We feel the name of the dolly she hopes is Molly
Fire glows red, on the mantelpiece I place a carrot and a slice of bread
For Santa Claus and his reindeer, Dad whisks me off to bed.

I hear all, from downstairs, grown ups enjoying themselves
As the Christmas pies are cooling, on the pantry shelves
Snow is deep, the carol singers are singing the hymns
Gran and Grampa are sitting reminiscing, with a glass of Pimms

The fanlight gives a shadow, passing was Santa Claus
In the living room so still, down the chimney presents pause
He asked the fairy, to sprinkle the elf's dust who said, 'If I must'
In the morning for Holly! The dolly called Molly! Given by trust.

Jan Ross

THE BROOKEDALE CLUB
(Dedicated to the ladies)

The Brookedale Club,
How could it be,
That you have stood hidden
Over 100 years from me?

Only male members,
No women allowed,
For we ladies are more than
Just a silent crowd.

Gentlemen, gentlemen,
You go too far,
Banning us ladies,
From the Bar.

Only male members
Allowed to play pool,
For are us, sweet ladies,
Allowed no rights at all?

For do you Brookedale Gentlemen,
Require it all,
For isn't it time for us ladies,
You learnt to play *ball?*

Sharon Tremlett

INFERTILITY

I never thought into the future,
held my mind in my hands.
Standing before that vast blue sea
I gazed,
feeling on the verge of existence.

Each new wave brought a new moment,
a new thought and feeling
to ebb over me
and sink down into a shell
on the warm sand behind.

Peace . . . because a glance
at the future horizon
showed sweeping blue
I knew would come into
the present.

It glimmered out of
the corner of my eye,
no need to look up
to check it were
untarnished . . .

But I never looked far enough
to see those plumped black clouds
waiting for me one day.
Blanketing my
dreams as yet unmade.

Jillian Shields

ALL ALONE

Soon be Christmas to behold
This story must be told
I'm last of the line, all alone
All I have is my telephone
Be a few calls on the day
'Happy Christmas' they will say
Quick to give all their news
Knowing full well, they won't amuse
May not have turkey, with all trimmings
Or a tree, with all its frillings
Least I'll have a nice warm home
Think of others, just streets to roam
What food will they have on the day?
Will they be able to keep cold at bay?
So I count my blessings, and I'll eat
My succulent chicken, and hot sweet.

I K Skinner

THE TRAMP

The tramp shifted restlessly in his cardboard box,
He pulled at the hole in one of his socks,
Found a dog-end in a pocketful of grime -
And his mind drifted back to another time.

There were two little faces smiling up at him,
Remembering this, his eyes filled to the brim.
Was there someone else standing there?
Her small, cool hands smoothing down his hair . . .

With these thoughts his body lay still
And sleep, so merciful, came until
This sad old man so tired and worn
Awoke to the sound of a London dawn.

Maureen Turner

NEIGHBOURS?

These people I meet
Seem so different to me,
In the way they talk,
And the funny way they walk,
And the funny way they dress.

Are they my neighbours
These people with their dark skins
And much darker eyes,
And voices that seem to shout
When they say the simplest things?

But wait a minute . . .
It was Lalti from next door
Looked after my wife and kids
When she was confined to bed
By unexpected illness!

And when she entered
A hard-to-reach hospital
It was Amritlal
From the next street who took me
In his car to visit her.

And just this morning
In this Home where I reside
My elevenses
Were brought by a dark-skinned lass
With a smile to light the world!

Dan Pugh

TRICK-OR-TREAT!

While I was trick-or-treating
One happy Hallowe'en,
I heard somebody shouting,
And rushed quickly to the scene.

A man had fallen in a stream,
The current took him under;
He was in need of rescuing,
To save him from his blunder.

He came back to the surface,
Where he floated more or less;
And then he yelled, 'Drop me a line!'
But what was his address?

At last I got him out, but
It's a good job I could swim;
As soon as I had pulled him out,
The blighter pushed me in!

Roger Williams

NOTHING BETTER TO DO!

A respectable lady heading for church
Walked with her friends every Sunday
When a pregnant unmarried girl walked by
It was the scandal for the village on Monday.

The following week this young girl went to church
And soon the gossip will be on them
'You good living folk, I played a wee joke'
And pulled out a cushion from under her hem!

Geraldine McMullan Doherty

THAT AUTUMN TIME OF YEAR
(Battle of the seasons)

Goodbye nice hot summer auf wiedersehen goodbye
The summer's off away now, the autumn it says, 'Hi.'
It's that autumn time of year now; the air is getting thin
It is slowly getting colder and the nights are drawing in
The flowers they all know it, they know they've had their day
They can't survive the coldness, they just die and blow away
It's that autumn time of year now; the birds all know this day
It is time for them to spread their wings and prepare to fly away
Fly away now birdies, you must go far away
To find a warmer place to live but please come back some day
It's that autumn time of year now; but the autumn, it's like thieves
Robbing us of summer's beauty like green leaves upon the trees
The trees they are all bare now, losers in the climate war
Standing there cold and naked with their leaves spread on the floor
It's that autumn time of year now; summer's beauty it must go
And even like in protest the grass just will not grow
It's that autumn time of year now; but I know it will not last
As in eight or nine months' time, summer comes back with a blast
The birds and flowers will return; of that you have no fear
So people don't get too upset at the *autumn time of year.*

M Strong

ANIMAL ANGST

Poor Mrs Vole had a very big mole,
stuck on the end of her nose,
she's a little bit weird,
with a full goatee beard,
and head butts wherever she goes.

Martine Jane Meah

NAN

My nan was all right, she was doing OK.
Then in less than a week, she was taken away.
All of a sudden I'm filled with shock and pain,
Filled with feelings that I couldn't possibly explain.
And this is shared by all who loved her so,
It's such a loss for us. We didn't want her to go.
But I've got to stop feeling so down and sad,
And start remembering all the good times we had.

I can remember bouncing around on Grampy's knee,
With Nan screaming at him to be careful with me.
I can remember the Kit Kats and the choc ices too,
'There's one for your sister and there's one for you.'
I can remember being bad and making her shout out loud,
Then wishing I'd been good and made my nan proud.
And as I got older she was still there for me,
Still filling me with chocolate and now cups of tea.

Then with children of my own, I saw more love pour out,
She'd stand up for them when they made me shout.
She'd always get down with them and have a play,
Always, loving, caring and full of funny things to say.
She's so easy to miss and so hard to let go,
There's things I want to tell her, things I want her to know.
But she knew we loved her and I hope that somehow
Nan's up there with Grampy, watching over us now.

Justin Stonell

THE SNOW QUEEN

See the Snow Queen - her gold crown
She looks so mean - with her cold frown

This is no dream - so please prepare
For her to freeze you with her stare

Watch her in her bright gold gown
For years she's ruled this old town

There's many a gnome - she's turned to stone
They take pride of place on her shelves
In her palace home and behind her throne
Also stand two stone-made elves
All alone and by themselves.

Watch her make her magic potion
To ice the stream - to freeze the ocean
She's no emotion - see her wicked beam
Please beware - of the Snow Queen!

P McIntyre

HALLOWE'EN

You dressing up like a monster,
brings out the Devil in you.

You scare me and then apologise too.
Your bad behaviour is excused
as today is Hallowe'en.

Hand-in-hand we will visit ten houses
but it seems like a hundred and two.

You're lucky as you have got many treats.

What will the dentist say?

Parveen K Saini

THE LAW OF THE KITCHEN

Two in a kitchen began to stir,
One was a 'he' and the other was 'her'.
They moved and then their bottoms clashed,
There followed the sound of broken glass.

Their work was stopped to clear up the mess,
She said it was his fault, she called him an ass.
She shouted at him, with all her might,
He was more tactful, avoided the fight.

An argument followed, she began to cry
To soothe her, he did his best to try.
Their first Sunday dinner, newly-weds they were,
But to share a kitchen, the danger was there.

He held her tightly in a loving embrace,
Grieved at seeing the tears roll down her face.
Then he discovered a smell, turned to espy,
The potatoes in the saucepan, had just boiled dry.

The lesson in this poem, don't push your luck,
A kitchen is only big enough, for one to cook.
In circumstances like this, the best you can do,
Is uncork a bottle and set glasses for two.

Make the kitchen your wife's personal domain,
Don't go in there unless to escape from the rain.
Make that the 'holy of holies', for safety's sake,
With food, leave it all, for your wife to bake.

Albert E Bird

HAVE YOU EVER

Have you ever
watched the sun at dawn
stopped to watch
a summer's morn?

Have you ever
sat watching
the waves on a shore
wishing the day would go on for evermore?

Have you ever
watched a field of corn
dancing in the breeze
dandelion heads floating
with tumbling ease?

Have you ever
watched a child at play
watched her sleeping
at the end of the day?

Have you ever
gazed at the stars at night
twinkling brightly
it's a wonderful sight!

These are things
that make me smile
and make me thank God
for being alive

A M Owen

WISHES

Wishes I think, are just thoughts in your head
Words that are there, though often not said
Wishes are things that can make life better
Like a call from a friend or a family letter
Wishes can make a rainy day brighter
Or a real heavy load seem so much lighter
Wishes can turn a dark night into day
Or make a bad dream, or a pain, go away
Wishes are often quite small tiny things
Like the movement of air by a butterfly's wings
Wishes quite often come straight from the heart
Most usually for good, that's the very best part
Wishes are made from one to another
Like the love of a child for its father or mother
The only things wrong with wishes I see
They're really just wishes, don't you agree?

H K Banks

THE ZOO

Monkeys jumping in their cage
Lions roaring in a rage
Tigers roaming on their land
Lovebirds sitting on your hand
Seals swimming in the pool
Doing tricks, looking cool
Gorillas eating a banana or two
The crocodile looking straight at you
Children playing on the swings
Hear the canaries as they sing
So much to see and do
A great day out at the zoo.

Claire Bloor

SEASIDE SCENE

Salt air, fresh and clean
Gulls swoop, dip and scream
Pebbles pink, grey, brown and blue
Another one to join the ice cream queue
Pushchairs carried to solid sand
Bucket and spade clutched in hand
Snoozing Auntie, under brolly bright
Uncle Bill unravelling string and kite
'Susan, catch,' a ball bounces near
Deckchairs lined up, along a painted pier
The day is almost out
Freckled faces pink, tired, pout
Pile into the car, shells, seaweed, buckets and balls
As daylight diminishes and night-time falls.

Maureen Keeble

NOT IN MY BACK YARD

Camouflaged against the debris
Lurk ragged, drab and crumbled lives
Cardboard is the bricks and mortar
Unnoticed homelessness here thrives

Urban scenes of deprivation
Blossoming with cursed misery
Shiver in the too-cold climate
Indifference and apathy

Shop doorways offer poor shelter
From revulsion's storm that rages
Wet and windy words a'splutter
From the mouths of *nimby* sages.

Kim Montia

MOTHER

The person that you've always known,
is the person that you've never known.
If only this person was here right now,
you'd have developed and have grown.

Is it that simple,
that some one has caused you grief?
Or is it your own doubt,
that's put you into disbelief?

Can it be quite easy,
to continue a life without another?
Or is it a constant hindrance,
to be without a mother?

I think that Mother sounds harsh,
as if she was ever so serious.
But without finding out,
what did she ever think of us.

You see her as ever laughing,
but that to you is dumb.
'Cause the last time you spoke,
you said 'Mummy' or maybe 'Mum'.

She is the centre of your life,
yet she's left so far outside.
I don't think she needs to be there,
and I don't think you need to hide.

Your mum is always with you,
and she'll be there every step of the way.
So start to understand her,
and live with her each day.

Keith Bennett

THE SILENT SCREAM

From my window I see the park
Today the weather is cold and stark
My eyes scan and find the beach
There with hands in pockets clench
It's hard to tell if he's young or old
All I know he is in the cold
Possessions around him, pickens are slim
As he hunts for food, in upturned bin
I talk with him at different times
Give food and money, what are his crimes?
I'll tell you he lives in our times
This caring country, aid given plentiful maybe
But what of others such as he
Care in the community they said was best
So it was put to the test
Then Government budgets cut like a knife
Causing the mentally ill and homeless so much strife
Those who need tender loving care
Rarely get it from anywhere
This lonely man is not alone
Many people have no home
Not wanted, crazies they are called
Laughed at, spat at, ridiculed
So much hope for them was promised
Everyone including Thomas
Every day he sits there
Looking like he hasn't a care
Just look into his eyes, see what I mean
Then maybe everyone will hear his silent scream

Jeanette Jackson

EXPENDABLE

The litter, like tumbleweed, passes by my door
in the orange glow of the street lamp
                        The alley cats sing their last note
                        and depart for home like satisfied revellers
Only strays look my way,
offended by my pungent odour

      Bitter irony that I, famished to within an inch of my life,
          Will in turn save so many creatures
      As, in desperation, they feed upon my swollen corpse

      People gaze through me as though through glass
          And try to disguise their obvious disgust

          But I don't mind - I don't moan
          I understand that I am expendable
          And none shall care when I go.

Amy McLaughlan (15)

A DIFFERENT WORLD

There's a different world that haunts our sleep
Kept inside our mind, all day, we keep
Fairy tales, dreams, magic and love
A stranded boat, with a message from a dove
Our own secret, of a place far away
Where hatred is lost and imaginations will play.

A dream of a world, of an exciting life
That could have been lost by the tip of a knife
Whenever we think that life is a bore
We can close our eyes and slip into our core
And dream of a place far, far away
Where we are able to do whatever we may.

Ali Collins

A Plea For Help

When we get to Heaven
Discover God above
Our troubles will be over
We find eternal love
This is what they tell me
As they feed me soup and bread
As I sit here in my cardboard box
With no roof above my head
They say that I'm redundant
But I still have to live
They're reducing staff, they don't need
The skills I have to give
No money left for food and rent
And so I have to go
I search - oh how I search for work
The answer - always no
When I get to Heaven
I hope that it is warm
That there is peace and kindness
And shelter from the storm
Until I reach that Heaven
I ask for what it is worth
Why? To enter God's kingdom
Must we suffer such hell upon Earth.

Lydia Barnett

Final Destination

Take my hand and join me on a trip you can't explain,
Cast your eyes on madness, that tangle with your brain.
Let me show you fantasies, beyond your wildest dreams,
In a land of colours, where nothing's as it seems.

Any place you want to go, I can take you there,
Raise your arms and slowly float up into the air.
Open your eyes and focus, the journey has begun,
Over the earth now you soar, up towards the sun.

Your mind takes flight, you wonder, what will wait you there,
Caring not for reasons, on what has brought you here.
There in bed below you, a part of you still lays,
Yet onwards and upwards still you fly, as if in a daze.

Mists and clouds before you, the journey's end is near,
The place that you have come to know, no man should fear.
Cup your ear and listen to what the spirit sings,
At last you're free, your soul's at rest, for God has given you wings.

Lindsay Kelly

THE WITCH

White is the glow of her long, narrow face,
Without blush or bloom of the air,
Whiter than the walls of an empty gallery,
Stripped of its art, oddly bare.

Eyes as cold as winter pools,
Darker than the curtain of night,
No sparkle of stars about them shone,
No edge of colour or light.

Ebony hair flowing down her back,
Glistening like a handful of jet,
Every curl, a cork-screw spin,
With the morning dew, appears wet.

Draped in sheets of silver,
Like a spider caught up in its thread,
Black is the widow among her,
Towering her victims, all dead.

Her voice surpasses the nightingale,
Much higher and distinctively clear,
Sending a chill of frost through the windowpane,
To fill tender dreams with fear.

She will never know the feeling of love,
Or the warmth and content of a smile,
Her touch only darkens the mind,
Her intentions, only wicked and vile.

Despite her gift of power,
To make frost destroy the fern,
She is forbidden the value of friendship,
Or to be loved by others in return.

Lottie Dolby

THE UMBRELLA OF LIFE
(Inspired by a majestic oak tree in St Wendreda's churchyard)

The umbrella of life is over my head
The day that it closes - I am dead.
It protects me through my time on Earth
It's been with me since the day of my birth
It takes the form of many things
From majestic trees to eagle's wings
From friends that are there in good times and bad
To my dogs that greet me and banish sad
From words that can tear emotions apart
To loving and caring that comes from the heart
From flowers in the garden that dance and sing
To the joy a tiny bird can bring
From the warmth and comfort in this home of mine
To my loved ones around me all of the time
From the sun in the morning to the moon at night
From a new day dawning to give such delight
This is the umbrella of my life
To live and enjoy as a mother and wife
One day I know my umbrella will close
When that will happen no one knows
Until then my umbrella will continue to hold -
My life - it's more precious than silver or gold

Maryska Carson

The Sea

The sea comes racing with a billowing roar,
Crashing then dying on the bleak, lonely shore.
You can sit and marvel and wonder how long
This never-ending onslaught has been going on.
Time passes slowly, days become years,
And still the rocks are sprinkled by the spray of the sea's salty tears.

As gentle as a mill pool, as meek as a lamb,
Or as rough and as wild as the tempest of an unleashed dam.
White foam horses dance gently on each wave as it draws near,
But the wind can blow them into a frenzy, causing the stoutest
                                                                heart to fear.

Crashing and roaring,
Slicing and pouring,
Endless and ceaseless, and so going on for evermore,
Over rock and beach, shingle and sand,
This wonder, the sea, never to obey mere mortal man's command.

Linda Davies

Stu's Curry

There was a young man called Stu,
Who wanted something to do.
So he cooked a curry,
Then ran in a hurry,
To spend all night in the loo!

Nicola Cobham

A BLESSING FOR LIZZIE

My dog, my dearest friend, is old now
And as the staring thought of death
Turns to look at me, I ask,
Am I ready for this loss?

Ready for the unstructured days
Without full stops or commas?
The empty house so ill at ease
Without her bark.
Toys no longer hunted and victoriously caught.

What will happen to my tears
She would wash so piously?
Who will keep them now
Zealously guarding them from me?

Her friend, the garden,
Lies in deepest shade.
The mighty trees bow their heads
As they protect their tiniest grave.

Dear Lizzie, walk with me once more
Proving death cannot hinder our affection.
Come with me through every closed door
As eternity gives us its benediction.

P Carleton

SILLY RHYME

River roads, railways and rhythm.
Sixpence, shillings, sailors and slime.
Tailors, tanners, tenors and time.
Oh what a silly rhyme.

Spanners, spoilers, spoons and spike.
Tickets, tellers, toners and ties.
Rine, riddles, rain and run.
Oh what a terrible rhyme.

Terrine, terror, terry and tease.
Vega, veg, veil and vein.
Wallaby, walls, wallet and walks.
Who made this rhyme?

Ant, apple, ask and an.
Bellows, balls, bats and boats.
Cats, cockles, collars and coats.
Oh my other rhyme.

Sponge, sugar, salt and scent.
Mum's my mixture and mop.
Dog's dinner, drovers and dents.
Oh this rhyme, will it make sense?

K Horsnell

STRESS

What is this thing that they call stress,
When all your life seems in a mess,
Your friends you think don't want to know,
Or if they do it doesn't show,
With real concern, and good intent,
But it's wasted time and effort spent,
You're in the doldrums, can't get out,
Makes you want to scream or shout,
Diminishes your confidence, raises your doubts,
That worthless feeling deep inside,
It's something that you just can't hide,
Shows in your walk and in your eye,
It's more like living with a lie,
That depressing ache of sad despair,
Even those you love can't share,
What does it take to shake this mood,
Brought on when you just sit and brood?
A friendly smile, a kind word said,
Something that will lift your head,
To realise life's not that mean,
And return again your self-esteem,
Once again, to pursue your dream.

B Foster

REMINDERS

People live and learn to like
Even when we hate it all.

Drawing straws to figure out
Which way our future goes
No one knows their own highs or lows.

Feelin' different with nothing done
Havin' lost you've really won.

All the reminders you didn't want
You've now got.
All the people you couldn't stand
Are sittin' around your table.
All the experience you've had so far
Have let you down.
Don't frown, happiness will come around.

I'm a soul with few words
But when something needs said I'll say it.
I'm quiet, I'm loud, renowned and proud
When someone needs help, I'll help.

S Cuthbert

HOPING FOR THE ROBIN'S RETURN

I had no need to go,
Outside in the snow,
Unlike the little robin,
Who came a-bobbin',
Braving cold feet,
In his need to eat.

With a hop and a skip,
He made the lawn trip,
To gratefully feed,
On my given seed,
Offering much rejoice,
In his finest voice.

This darling bird,
Had my heart stirred,
Making this day of white,
All golden and bright,
And this feeling lingered on,
Long after he was gone.

For the seed I had laid,
I was handsomely repaid,
So I now have need to go,
Outside in the snow,
For I'm hoping he will repay,
The seed I intend to lay.

Donna June Clift

Sunday At My Gran's

We used to go to Grandma's on Sunday for our tea
My mum, my dad and sisters, my brother Ray and me
Fred was drinking in the 'Crown' at least 'til half-past three
While working in the kitchen was my old gran, Gertie
Fred rode home upon his bike with ice cream and sweets
Then off to bed to have a sleep beneath the nice clean sheets
'Be quiet kids,' my mother said, 'your grandad, he's in bed
If you do not behave yourselves, I'll clip you round the head.'
Our tea was almost ready now, the table all set out
'Your tea is on the table, Fred,' my grandma used to shout
There were different sandwiches all made with different things
We all sat and had our fill and felt like we were kings
There was fruit and jelly, the ice cream from the shop
Different cakes and biscuits, there surely was a lot
After tea we all sat down, huddled by Grandad's feet
Sitting, hoping patiently for a sugared almond sweet
Those memories still linger here, though it has been a while
Remembering Sunday at my gran's will always make me smile

Stephen Frederick Burns

THE BUTTERFLY . . .

The sweet little butterfly is a joy to see,
His wings soft like velvet giving beauty to me,
The colours so radiant when he's flying about,
Chasing each other with no worry or doubt.

The lightness he has when he's high in the sky,
Not a sound does he make, you never hear him cry,
Fluttering around the flowers in bloom,
Enjoying the fragrances, enchanting like the moon.

This tiny small creature gives pleasure to all,
He is so very graceful and we are so tall,
To be like a butterfly with beauty and grace,
A heavenly creature, Mother Nature takes her place.

Janet Brook

I'M SORRY

Hayley, it was you that I was infatuated
With Ian I loved and related
You are both my inspiration for fighting
Giving a different perspective, a different sighting

Ian, the pressure I put on you I regret
Because I regard you as the best friend I've met
I could never tell this to your face
Now I'm healed without a trace

I want to turn back time like when we used to be
Blazing the bay in curiosity
Those special times from one day to another
Now I don't see you, I miss you like a brother

John Lee

Morning After 2

To keep us safe from fireworks
Dad had a barrier set.
Mary could not bob for apples.
Her face and hair were wet.
We searched for the treasure hunt,
Found a prize at every spot.
As it was getting chilly
Mother gave us something hot.
Baked potatoes, hot chocolate.
We sat together on the path
Dad started the fireworks.
We could see our steamy breath.

We cheered as every rocket went;
Held sparklers in our hands.
It was nearly midnight, the fun
Must end. Down with wands.
Tired, breathless, we said goodbye.
Up the stairs we trod.
Dressing clothes flung on the floor.
Soon in the land of Nod.

Jane England

I Awoke But Did I?

One day I awoke to find myself lying on the ground
I looked up, there were leaves all around
It was cold but quiet, not one little sound
It was dark but dry. Where am I?
Up I stood to have a closer look
There were trees above and mud beneath
There was a dim light way ahead and something old like a shed
I crept forward very slow, for what was watching me I did not know
I could hear the sound of the leaves under my feet
As my heart would miss a beat
Creeping towards the shed I heard a sound
I turned my back to look around
But there I was stood by the door
I felt something move on the floor
Then a hand touched my head
There had to be something in that shed
Too scared to even turn around
I slung my body to the ground
I tried to crawl and get away
But will I ever? I can't say
Am I here? I don't know
If I am please let me go
Am I awake or am I not?

Maria Jayne Halliday

PERSPECTIVE

Tranquil Trouville
Lapped by the whirling waves,
Weaving foamy flowers
Out of the receding sea;
Shaded, oiled, cushioned
The rich reclined;
Lower-priced folk
Proffered themselves
As whole-burnt offerings.

I shook my indolent limbs free
And walked far out
Beyond child call
Beyond gull call
Over the smooth beach
Out of touch
Out of reach
Of the sun-winning mass,
Who at a generous distance
Became as blobs on an impressionist canvas.

Mary Frances Mooney

OF AZTECS AND CONQUISTADORS
(The Aztec people knew themselves as 'The México'
'Have you grown weary of your servants?
Are you angry with your servants? O Giver of Life?' - Aztec poem)

On giant ships they came from a land across the sea,
And the people of the México wondered who these men might be.
They rode upon strange beasts whose coming shook the earth.
And Moctezuma welcomed them, assuming Quetzalcóatl's
                                  promised rebirth.
For the Aztec king was mindful of ancient prophecy,
Which told of the return of the ancient God who would arrive by sea.
'Was this the realisation of the prophecy?' asked the Aztec king
And if this was Quetzalcóatl, what new wonders would he bring?
But these were no returning deities, and he would soon regret
                                  his decision
To welcome these men as ancient gods, for they had a
                                  treacherous mission.
Cortés was not the God of prophecy, he came in search of Aztec gold,
And soon the Aztec king would know this was not the god of old.

The people of the México gave all they had and more,
But the greed of the conquistadors led to inevitable war.
Soon the seeds of suspicion grew and the uneasy peace gave way,
The people of the México sought to drive the invaders away.
But the invaders had the upper hand, their weapons were too strong,
And they joined with the Aztec's enemies, their victory did
                                  not take long.
Moctezuma passed unto the heavens, his son died of the
                                  Spanish disease,
And those not killed by the invader's swords were brought by
                                  smallpox to their knees.
So Cuauhtémoc, the last Aztec emperor, made his final stand,
And was taken prisoner and ignominiously hanged.
So perished the Aztec empire, though the story is told,
Of how the Spanish were thwarted by the people who hid away
                                  all the remaining gold!

So they laid to waste the beauty that had been the Aztec capital city,
And within the walls of Tenochtitlán the invaders showed no pity.
Throughout the lands of the Méxica, the conquistadors waged their war,
Until, in less than two whole years, the Aztec empire was no more.
Great cities lost, people slain, a thriving civilisation gone,
All for the greed of those wanted the metal that shone as the sun.
Many years would pass, many suns would set, until the people
                                                                rose again,
To drive out the invaders and become, once more, free men.
Though all that stood of ancient times were the ruins of the past,
They fought and were victorious and became a free nation at last.
And for their newborn country they took a name from long ago,
In honour of the long dead Méxica, they called it México!

Juan Pablo Jalisco

ELVER HARVEST

Shadows walk the bank
with lanterns and Heals' netting
To take from the ever running
silverene stream

The Easter harvest, heritage food
now sadly destined for other mouths
No longer hawked at doors in pint glasses
with street cries or towelled chairs outside houses

A birthright legacy taken
by efficient trawlers and 'the station'
Catchers of fish and men alike
bespoilers of the future

Greedily carrying tomorrow's harvest
in their exporting exploiting tankers
Bought from Judas fools with no
thought for generations yet unborn!

Martin Blakemore Davis

NATURE'S BLESSINGS

If the winter months hae got ye doon
Wi the cauld and frost and snaw,
Ah can tell ye o' a simple wie
Tae cast yer blues awa',
Tak a walk intae the country
And soak up the joys o' spring,
There's a wealth o' things tae see and hear
And it disnae cost a thing.
Stond and listen tae a lerick
As it dithers up abuin'
Or the singin' o' a linet
Fae a patch o' floorin' brim
Or the hauntin' lilten whistle
Fae a bleckie on the rowan
The chorus o' thae singin' birds
Must smooth awa' yer frown
Ye'll see bobbin' tails o' rabbits
As ye walk around a turn
Or a startled shoal o' minnies
As yer shaddae hits the burn
And there awa roond aboot ye
Even doon amongst yer feet
There's flowers o' every shape and colour
That ye'll no see on a street
So tak a guid look roond aboot ye
And enjoy the things ye see
For maybe in a year or twa
They'll a' hae disappeared.

Henry Crawford

FOR MY HONEY
(Dedicated to Venesha)

This poem is for my baby - my honey.
The one that I love to hug and to hold.
The one who I want to kiss daily.
Whose name is forever written on my heart in gold.

You are the one that I wished for.
You love me as much as I love you.
You are the only woman that I do adore.
I see myself with no one other than you.

I want to spend my life with you.
I want to be always at your side.
I hope that you want to be with me too.
There's no one else I wish to find.

Me and you will last forever.
Me and you will have loads of days just having fun.
Me and you will strive to endeavour through all our troubles.
You and me will grow and become one.

Baby I love you more than words have justice to say.
I know you believe me when I say my heart is true.
Baby I long for you every hour of every day.
I have, I do and I always will be dangerously in love with you.

Daniel Jones Jr

THE SILVERED GLASSY SEA

There's a mountain starkly rising
From the silvered glassy sea
With a penetrating hole high up
Where a hole should never be;
What mystery has conspired thus
To leave it gaping there?
Did only savage weather
Leave it far beyond repair?

The North Sea's spirit tells us
When the moon shines full and bright
At the spot where through the hole it shines
You'll spy the awesome sight
Of a ghostly ghastly three mast ship
On that silvered glassy sea
Driven along by an unseen gale
Never destined to be free.

So stay clear of that mountain
When the night is cold and still
And the moon is low yet fully formed
In the grip of winter's chill
Lest you glimpse it through the gaping hole
Where a hole should never be,
For you'll not outrun that ghostly craft
On the silvered glassy sea.

Ian C Gray

ETERNAL EYE OF GIBRALTAR

We hopped on a cruiser at Napoli dock,
Surprisingly, also afire.
On route to Gibraltar's covert Sir Deadlock,
Our listening post for the wire.

Such quaint little people, fixed on sovereignty;
No thought of the larger action.
Our old bugger London was guard on duty,
At this global telex station.

Psychology staff numbered more than our troop,
Vast numbers for census fact teams.
All persons, regardless, were placed in a group,
And ranked into officious schemes.

Our data immense, we drew accurate maps;
Tried adding radiography.
Our methods and tools guaranteed our long zaps,
Regardless of geography.

Intelligence grew, and progressed, as before;
Yet, somehow the focus had changed.
No longer was talk of the rights of the poor;
But, how malleable they ranged.

The island's quaint little people had wireless,
Antennae, ruddy teletype.
It may be that all cultures crave such excess;
The time for cheapened life was ripe.

Anthony M Blackwell

RIVER TYNE

River Tyne, main artery of the northern border.
Its course scoured out by advancing glaciers millennia ago.
After they had receded, painted warriors came.

From across the sea, bringing their gods with them;
To settle on its banks; to hunt and fish its peat-stained waters.
Many centuries later, Agricola; Roman general,

With his legions, in his quest to conquer the Caledonians;
Braved its flow. The last millennium, forded by English
And Scottish kings and queens, in their north or

South thirst for power. One of its violent periods;
The 16th Century, sometimes carried the blood
Of moss troopers down to the sea.
Nowadays, it carries the laughter of children
Playing in its shallows on a warm summer's day.

Les Davey

UNTITLED

There's welcome in the firelight glow
When duty's done, to rest awhile,
And as the varied thoughts overflow
They bring content with naught of guile.

The chosen books are near at hand
Which never fail their joys to share
And music with enchanting wand
Both touch and add those moments rare.

Each picture doth a memory raise
That seems to open a window wide
This which the conjured family strays
Returning as upon the tide.

D G Douglas

SISTINE SONNET

As a child young Buonaroti ran wild
Second son of the Mayor of Caprece
With no mother his youth was uneasy
The beauty of marble had him beguiled

At age sixteen he carved a clever fake
It was purchased by Cardinal Riario
Angelo, in a happy scenario
Was offered work in his first lucky break

Pursued by the Pope's irate descendants
And delayed by his lazy contractors
Half his efforts he considered waste

With sponging relations and dependants
Distracted by war and other factors
He continued to carve in unabated haste.

Bill Looker

MOTHER

As each year goes by,
I shed a tear, o' Lord,
When you took my mother from me,
It seems like only yesterday
That she was here with me,
O' Lord, you broke my heart
She was my guardian angel,
Perfect in every way,
My heart is broken into pieces,
And never can be mended,
O' Lord take care of my mother
For me, and keep her safe
In your arms for me.

Garth Evans

MEMORIES

We all have lots of memories,
Both good and bad.
Some that make us happy,
And some that make us sad.

Memories of our childhoods,
Some more recent too.
The memories I will cherish,
Are those involving you.

The memory of our first meeting
And my first date with you.
Our picnic on that Sunday
When my love was new.

Our evenings spent together,
And the lovely summer weather.
Lying together, watching you sleep,
Things that make my love so deep.

We haven't known each other long
But I could write a book,
Of all the lovely memories
I have since that first look.

Over the times that are to come
I'm sure that we will have,
More wonderful things to share,
More ways to show how much I care.

I Horwell

Doctor's Surgery

Good morning Mrs Brown - please sit down
Tell me your symptoms that's a start
I keep having these headaches
At least two a day
I keep taking the painkillers to keep them at bay
Do you work - are you under stress?
As my patient no need to undress
I'll take your blood pressure
To see what I can find
Nothing unusual - it's all in the mind
I'll prescribe some placebos and come back next week
We'll find out if you're a mental freak
He had a phone call the other day
To hear Mrs Brown had passed away.

Marilyn Hine

The Old Car Boot

I love to go down to our old car boot
To walk round and round all the tables
Then decide just what to buy
A bargain here, a bargain there
Oh what shall I buy?
Kettles, teapots, old saucepans too
Shoes, two big shoes, two small
Books and games, puzzles galore
Oh what shall I buy?
A bargain is a bargain all said and done
So I must buy things before they shut
I buy a jigsaw here, a toy dog there
Books and comics here and there
Oh what good bargains I got today
From our old car boot sale

Ella Wright

WAS GOD A TIME TRAVELLER

As I look into the night sky
At the stars sparkling brightly
Is God the all-seeing eye
Does he really hold the key?

Is he really the supreme being
Or a time traveller from another dimension
Have I the right in questioning
The existence of His translation?

Is Earth the birthplace of Eden
Or is this a universal laboratory
Where we are rats in its garden
And God is an alien on a religious journey.

Surely we're not the only congenial source
Intelligent life in this universal solar system.
There could even be an ascension force
Celestial bodies waiting to bid us welcome.

Not even for one minute do I believe
We're the only entity
I find it hard perhaps a little naive
That God's theology is His sole legacy.

Did God send forth a giant fireball
To a dark distant planet called Earth
Where the purity of Genesis did install
Life for all it was worth?

And thus through the ashes life was born
This I think was the origin
The creation of many a different form
Where do we go from here I can only imagine.

Walter Mottram

MY DADDY

Our time was short,
Jesus knew you were tired,
He said come to me,
Your memory left me inspired.

I will now go on,
Without my best friend,
But your love still surrounds us,
There really is no end.

So goodbye Daddy,
Life isn't always fair,
At this given moment,
It is too much to bare.

I wish I did not have this ache,
I feel as though my heart will break.

As you now go on your journey,
And I must go on alone.
I know you are all around me,
You will always be in our home.

When that soft breeze,
Blows gently through my hair,
I will know it's you Daddy,
Telling me you still care.

S P Cockayne

REDUNDANCY

For forty-odd years I had worked, all the time,
I thought, an achievement this service of mine!
For I'd never been sacked, nor put on the dole,
   I looked on myself as a busy old soul,
   Responsible - diligent - honest. In fact,
Just ev'rything bosses could come to expect.

But all are dispensable - this is the truth,
For those of long service and, equally, youth.
My end came so fast, like a huge thunderclap,
'I'm sorry to say - you're redundant old chap!'
Though time has elapsed, can't believe it still,
For me, I'm afraid, this was some bitter pill.

Recession brings problems for all of we folk
And troubles hang heavy - like gigantic yoke.
Those last in employment were, mostly, first out,
That true dedication was honoured, don't doubt -
No longer the case, things are looking so black,
We're just 'numbers' together, on the same track!

The *personal* aspect, has gone by the board,
Allegiance counts zero; for this - no reward!

L Alan Johnson

BELONGING - THE WAY WE ARE
*(This poem is dedicated to the Anglian Church
in their search for a Christian acceptance of all people as they are)*

I loved a friend,
our closeness made us one.
Close in our thoughts and way of life,
therefore bodily too.

My friend loved me,
constant in his trust.
We drew together, and so stayed,
but others did not comprehend.

Sensual was our bond,
that first declaration of heart's love.
But time has settled our desire
into true, platonic compact.

Love is still there,
unrecognised in critical view,
but ever close and true, my friend.
Still I love you.

Yet, I also love another.
Supreme our hearts to rule.
My Lord knows all about us
and unites His people, all.

Jo Allen

UNTITLED

Why is it when I'm looking
I simply cannot find
The batch of poems
I would like to submit
Winning a competition in mind.

When will I be tidy
Organised to seek
Will it take but just one day
Or maybe a whole week.

Am I having senior moments
What will become of me
I so wanted to succeed in life
It's all such a puzzle you see.

Oh well so far to date
I cannot prove my case
So I'll admit defeat just this once,
To truly seal my fate.

One day when I'm discovered
Then I alone can tell
I'm not a mixed up senior
In my mind I'm still just a gell!

Jacky Edwards

MISSION TO MARS

'Seventy times seven': an order to forgive men without stint,
Impossible number to take on board in Christ's Jerusalem.
Sixty thousand, twenty two two eight seven,
We're more numerate in a computer age.

'The God of war is close by' in our twenty-first century,
Closer than he's ever been since the coming of man,
Closer than he'll be for more than twenty thousand years
And another Darwinian echo of far islands.

An army of men have set up optical instruments
To track the colour of blood, seen with the naked eye.
They will monitor probic descent from a capsule ('fridge-sized',
A modern convenience implicated in our planet's destruction)

And there will be 'Mars-gazing parties with barbecues'.

But what need have we of blood from another planet,
Another God of war? Fathers of families here
See hope of paradise killing unknowing children
Of other men they call enemies.

Armies of blood-letters stalk our uneasy world,
And 'human remains' are discovered in suicide trucks.
'The war to end wars' was to be 'over by Christmas'.
Now without end there is 'war and rumours of war'.

Gold glittering globes, lit branches, frantic tills
Will coincide with an intrusive shaft, dog-carried
To investigate large areas for future conflict.
Will coincide with 'peace on Earth', 'goodwill' and other lies.

And the gods of war spread wider their envenomed wings.

Maureen Carr

A Friday Walk

'Not another stile,' came the cry
Arms and eyes went up to the sky
'When will all this climbing end?'
'Not long, the finish is just round the bend!'

We started that morning with the sky blue and bright
Conditions, for walking, with a breeze, were just right
Onward and upward is the order of the day
Follow your leader, he knows the way.

Over the first stile and into a bog
Someone's quite kindly made a path from a log
Soon we're all over and off up the hill
Got to keep going, where there's a way there's a will

There's a good way ahead and the going's all right
The signs that guide us are yellow and bright
There are new stiles ahead and footbridges too
To help us cross streams and fields full of goo

Across the field, there's a bull up ahead
With a ring in his nose so that he can be led
He's no trouble today, there are cows all around
He's happy and peaceful asleep on the ground

There's a trig point ahead, the top of the hill
We rest for a while, then off 'cause there's still
A way to go 'til we stop for our lunch
We're off down the hill, all of a bunch

We're making good time when it starts to rain
We get all geared up, but it's not the same
Never mind, it's not far to the pub
A couple of pints and a plateful of grub

The food is good and the service is great
Whatever we want, we don't have to wait
We're soon all finished and have had our fill
When we're ready to go we'll pay at the till

The rain's gone away, it'll dry in a while
In the meantime we'll start with a stile
From now to the end there's stiles galore
Over one and there's more and there's more

Through the woods and over a bridge
Up a rise and over the ridge
Across the road and over a stile
Makes a change, hasn't been one for a while

Across a field that once held a bull
Up a slight rise, not much of a pull
Along a lane, it's not very far
Up another rise and we're back to the car.

Trevor Headley

SAVE OUR TREE

A big old tree stands by our house, just blowing to and fro,
It's been stood there for many a year, I'd hate to see it go,
When I was small I used to climb our tree, right to the top,
But then my mum would catch me, her heart would nearly stop!
It shades us in the summertime, so we don't get too hot,
And shields us in the winter, like a baby in his cot,
Springtime is the best of all, when our tree starts to bloom,
It takes away the misery, boredom and the gloom,
So have a heart before you start chopping at our tree,
There's much more to it than you think, a lot more than you see,
In autumn time the leaves all fall, and turn our garden brown,
We love our tree, it's dear to me, please don't chop it down.

Ann M Crampton

HOLIDAY ISLAND

Yes we are having fun
On this island in the sun,
One should think it's like Heaven
But it all kicks off at seven.
The mixer starts up,
There's hammers and drills,
We start taking our pills.
We've come for a rest
Get some sun on our chest,
We couldn't ask for more
Our hair's gone like straw,
Yes we are having fun
We can cope with the sun
It's the bites and the piles
We seem to have walked miles.
But when all's said and done
We love our island in the sun.

Eileen Robinson

THE LOVE

The love I hear so much about
Has come for me
In the image of you
And unhinged me
That image of you
My love - my beautiful destroyer
Dark angel that you are
You've come for me
Undone and unstitched me
I am no longer -
Master of the helm, captain of the ship,
I am no longer . . . me.

D Salter

STOKE ON WHERE?

The terraced rows, once stood real tall
where children played, against grey wall.
Down long, old cobbled streets we walked
when people laughed and neighbours talked.

Remembering how, for Dad, I'd wait,
outside those cold, old foundry gates.
For a few odd coppers, from his wage,
so oft, wish I, could turn back page.

This town, strange, only few have heard
whose precious wares, once graced the world.
Some once proud jewel in Stafford's knot
a place somehow, seems time forgot.

This modern tale of saddened Stoke
where her bottle kilns, no longer smoke
The potter's wheel, no more can turn
and the factory chimneys, fail to burn.

Much more than a city, we are five towns
feels such a waste, they closed us down.

Steve Rushton

RAINBOWS

The threads of light, against the darkness,
the patterns of colour, against the grey,
we need the one, to know the other,
today, tomorrow . . . every day.

Weaving of the joy, through sorrow,
showing sunshine, after rain,
making rainbows, through the cloud cover,
today, tomorrow, every day.

Helen McLellan

OUR WONDERFUL COUNTRYSIDE

See the tree how tall
And the bush how wide
See the colour of the blossom
Our wonderful countryside

See the ripple of the river
And watch the squirrels hide
See the petals of forest flowers
Our wonderful countryside

Now close your eyes and see the truth
The miles of concrete that astride
Where have all the flowers gone
In our wonderful countryside

Now turn around and look to the sky
Behind bellowing smoke and the sun does hide
With acid rain and pollute streams
See our wonderful countryside

The trees now gone and the land laid bare
Not much life now does abide
The view now nothing to years ago
Of our wonderful countryside

The farmer now long since passed
The house and stock pushed aside
It's only greedy people that have ruined
Our wonderful countryside.

Richard Trezise

THE POTTERIES
(A place called Stoke
Dedicated to James Jerves - Staffordshire Regiment)

Once upon a time in a place called Stoke
    The sky was lit by fire
And the air was filled with smoke

Chimneys shaped like bottles
    Were furnaces burning hot
In went the clay
    And out came a pot

By the likes of Wedgewood, Doulton, Moorcroft and Wade
    For the world this was where, pottery was made.
Day and night the fires burned non stop
    Boxes, crates and horses' carts
Pots, stacked high to the top

In this place of production
    The work it was non stop
With famous names known world-wide
    It's quality hard to top

Ovens alight and well ablaze
    The city black in smoke
There were no fog free days
    For the people of smoggy Stoke

Today the bottle ovens
    How they all stand cold
All the secrets of the craft in Stoke
    They are gone to the days of old.

Steve Jervis-Price

THE PHANTOM

As night falls with darkened sky,
Lingering shadows fall close by.
And whilst the moon drapes clouds around,
A phantom stirs pronouncing sound.

Stealthily creeping with hush and calm,
Now noisily seeping with strange alarm.
Suddenly dashing fierce and wild,
In tempest clad mantle with tossing styled.

He gallops along down harnessed hedges,
Down grassy slopes like racing sledges.
Through quaking bushes to the quivering pond,
Spraying the lilies and willows beyond.

He rattles loose chatter on battered old doors,
Breathes fierce fiery whistles on dark dank bleak moors.
Makes dilemma his goal for each new reception,
Ploughing the night in his cloak of deception.

And as he visits with taunting cries,
The church and its graves he still defies.
The plight of loved ones forever gone,
With dust and leaves and then moves on.

He traces his every step time and time again,
But somehow his movements seem all in vain.
As night becomes dawn and dawn becomes day,
The phantom steals now gracefully away.

Peter W Hodgkins

MY SOUL

Locked away within my soul where no one else can see
There is a very special place, a secret part of me
It's the heart of my emotions, the centre of my life
It sends the tears into my eyes in times of joy or strife
It puts a smile upon my lips each time I look at you
It makes me glow with tender love, a love so strong and true
This love will last forever, I know that this will be
For you are in that secret place that's deep inside of me.

You have become my heart's emotions, heartache, joy and pain
You are the laughter bubbling when I'm walking in the rain
You are the teardrops falling when I'm hurt and want to cry
You are my source of comfort when my chances pass me by
You are my only helping hand along life's narrow way
You are the path I walk upon, the pillow where I lay
You're there forever darling and I'll always love you so
Because you are my very soul, I'll never let you go

Kay Hope

A LOOK AT LIFE

A gentle breeze
Thro' twisted bough
A silent moan
So here, so now
A look at life
Thro' furrowed brow
A chance to smile
To weep, to bow
It's life we serve
So here, so now.

W Kershaw

LOST THEN FOUND

As life was passing me by each day,
I'd lay in bed and I would say,
'I'm so lonely I'm so blue,'
then sweet Peter I found you.
You took me out, we fell in love,
so I thank God up above.
I never thought that I would find,
someone who treated me so kind.
You help me get through every day,
you help to take the pain away.
I have to say a big thank you,
because I now do not feel blue.
All I feel is love in my heart
and I know we will never part.
So Peter please stay and never leave,
because I know that you believe.
That we will soon be husband and wife,
and stay together all our lives.

Jean Hargreaves

THE BAG LADY

Sitting here watching the world go by
Could be quite a pleasant distraction
If my stomach was full and my shoulders were dry
And my smile got a friendly reaction

If the soles of my feet had some shoe on
And my hands were not permanent black
I could get up before they had dew on
And apply for the things that I lack

But it's hard to find good motivation
When you can't see the wood for the trees
And I only cause slight consternation
When I'm begging here down on my knees

I don't ask for a lot, just a chance to be me
And a place I can lay down my head
My skills are not needed; I'm useless, you see
I'm too old now for learning, 'they' said

If I had half a chance, I could learn a new trade
Though my fingers are stiff now and sore
It's with spending long hours at a loom in the mill
And through sleeping too long on the floor

I could go to the seaside, or maybe The Lakes
But the people there frown even more
I compete with the birds for the crumbs and the cake
That folk throw out, too stale, from their door

Don't feel sorry for me, 'cos I'm used to it now
But please give me a smile when you pass
The summers are warm but the winters are long
I was happy when I was a lass

Jane Hewitt

IMAGES M

Thou fledst from me that sometime did me seek
And took with thee the balm that soothed my wounds;
The tortured axis of a mind too weak
Convulsed without these in the sunless noons.

But day by day with each new-practised skill
I sensed the nature of my love for thee;
Yet nursed a melancholy yearning still
Which thy sweet presence can alone set free.

As moth toward the dazzling light still drawn
And fluttering in unseemly panic die:
My sacrifice to thee and children born
Who journey freely in a cloudless sky.

Lo, thus, in ecstasy, despair and pain
My distillated passion starved again.

Victor Church

BUTTERFLY TREE

Buddleia, buddleia, buddleia tree,
Oh what pleasures you bring me,
I could sit and watch for hours,
As butterflies danced upon your flowers.

Red admirals, a cabbage white,
And tortoiseshells are a beautiful sight.
The sunshine feels warm upon my face,
All the garden flowers, I love this place.

Birds sing below the clear blue sky,
There, another butterfly, flutters by.
I know the summer will soon be gone,
But butterfly memories will live on.

Joe Wood

BE MINE

You are so sweet from your
Head to your feet
You are so beautiful and kind
Sweetheart you're always in my mind
You have a warm caring smile
That I could lock up on your file
You are so perfect and sweet
I would love to make a meet
You have a sweet soft face
That no one on Earth can replace
You have soft skin like a baby
And maybe we can be together
Through all sorts of weather
I would like to keep you warm
Through the cold scary thunderstorm
So baby please will you be mine
Until the end of all time
Darling sweetheart be mine

Carol Mary Woods

MY PRIDE, MY JOY

I remember the day that you were born,
my precious gift was a baby boy.
The face of an angel and eyes so blue
I thanked the Lord for giving me you.

I named you Kieron, the special one,
a bond so close, just you and your mum.

I watched you grow, now a young man,
you've had your share of ups and downs.

But one thing Kieron I want you to know,
the price you are now paying is very low.

There is only one judge at the end of the day,
he'll treat you fair, let you have your say
So my son, there is just one thing left to say,
'You are my pride, my joy till my dying day
lots of love as always Mum xxx.

Mary McKeeve Moore

Janling Sichel

Janling now lives in a safe, sheltered place,
    How private, secluded, I cannot yet tell.
But I know that my niece with the beautiful face
    Lives quite near the Rembrandt Hotel.

If only that Rembrandt could call on my niece,
    If only he glimpsed her sweet face,
If only he painted her all in one piece -
    To exhibit her all over the place!

While he sent such a picture to hang in the Tate,
    He could paint a copy to hang in my room,
But this is the difference of fortune and fate -
    Van Rijn Rembrandt lies long in his tomb.

But what is a picture compared to true life,
    What value has matter to mind?
Like richness of spirit which overcomes strife,
    The soul is supreme in mankind.

As Janling is soulful and full of life's zeal,
    With no Rembrandt to paint her bright face,
Her uncle will find her to see if she's real,
    To know how she grows with such grace.

Brian Dilworth

A Ring Around The Basin

The waving grass, all tall and proud,
The blue, blue sky, without a cloud,
The stony path goes on and on,
The strong sea wall, we walk upon.

The thorny brambles, dark and sharp,
The running dog, with piercing bark,
The sea, withdrawing from the sand,
The worms stretch up, like rubber bands.

The tea-room, with its pristine pine,
The fisherman, with rod and line,
The 'Jolly Sailor', the 'Ship's' big rival,
The gulls and terns fight for survival.

The 'Barbie' boats, all mauve and pink,
The canal barge, with kitchen sink,
The lock, gates closed, full to the brim,
The big yachts, with their sails all trimmed.

The 'Daisy meadow', full of cars,
The recycling bins, full of bottles and jars,
The fishermen's cottages, tidy and neat,
The old school house, the long main street.

The bus shelter, come football goal,
The local children, large and small,
The boy next door, with missing shoe,
The pavements, spoiled by doggy do!

The pump house, and church of St George,
The alleyway, leads to our door,
The last sight of water, as waves spit foam,
The house, we love to call our home.

Wendy Smith

Perhaps I Should Have Spoken Up Sooner

I bought myself a parrot, a proper little corker,
On the understanding it was a superb talker.
But as days went by and not a word, to the pet shop I did pass,
And on their suggestion, bought it a looking glass.

Another week, and still no word. To the pet shop who had had her,
I went to complain - heard them explain, it should have a little ladder.
So this I got, and home did trot, but still no sound was heard,
Off to the shop, very angry now, to complain about this bird.

They calmed me down, and listened to my trial and tribulation.
Suggesting I should buy a swing to give it stimulation.
A few days later, the poor thing died. In its cage I heard it drop,
But at last it spoke, I heard it gasp,
                'Don't they sell any food in that shop?'

A G Revill

Freedom

Seems as if it's gone too far,
Life behind a metal bar,
Hearing the birds twitter out there,
Life can be so unfair.
As the light shines upon half his face,
His dark memory haunts his race.
Never before has he seen such a sight,
Where the dogs come behind and give others a fright,
Long and sharp,
Hard and rough.
Painful marks hurts is stuff.
As one day ends another begins.
He eats out of rusty tins.

Saleem Tariq

MY DREAM

When I saw you last night
I knew it was a dream
You were standing there
Looking all serene
You smiled a smile I won't forget
It was that smile when we first met
You cross'd the floor stood by my side
You held my hand I almost cried
It was just like it used to be
I thought you had come back to me
That smile you smiled across the floor
Made me want you all the more
If only dreams could come true
I'd like to spend them all with you

Gerald T Western

MODERN AND ANCIENT - CONTINUED

From childhood it has stood the test
In school and college, too
Stored loads of information
As I the past review.

From I awake until I sleep
My brain is daily used
A very needful part of me
Which must not be abused.

There are many lovely memories
Stored for future pleasure
As well as useful knowledge
And each a precious treasure.

Nell Thompson

BUILDING ON BELIEF

My cart of hand picked flints was sold, I thought to head off home
But an inner voice did tell me, *'your work is not yet done'*.
I joined the men from near and far, we toiled from dawn 'til dusk,
Digging trenches, hauling stones and making mortar dust.
I marked my nearing birthdate by lashing scaffolds tall,
My coming years I measured high upon the growing walls.
I faced each stone and placed each stone and never did I flinch
For I was driven onwards as I laid each unique flint.
Gifts from Earth and forest raised to Him on high
Humble stone and wood and bone, nothing was denied.

Men who worked around me from youths to sinewed old,
Shared the lift of spirit as our sweat damped wood and stone.
Climb the rising tower, roof the chancel tall, carve the door and pave
The floor with care and love and awe.
Raise statues to our Saviour, gild the Saints on high
Though we could not buy our holy space and under altar lie,
Reservations for the privileged more worthy than the low,
Whose position, wealth and power denied the need to know
We of faith and fortitude who raised the building heavenward
With eyes that saw and ears that heard yet could not read a single word.

The bells toll for all time. Faith fades and grows too thin,
Though the church in which I gave my best is much the same within.
My sweat and tears are dry now, centuries passed by,
Workmanship is all that is left to mark the question *why?*
A tower clawing skyward for answers from above,
Millennia of insight, divisions, guidance . . . love.
I who dug stones and carted wood and washed them with my breath
Rose upward on the drift of prayer and welcomed my own death,
Believing humble effort would shape the world to come,
Yet still the bells speak out His words, *'My work is not yet done . . .'*

Linda Preece

SHE

She didn't choose to walk alone
She didn't want to look to the ground
She didn't choose to be a mute
She didn't choose to hear no sound
It's the only way she knows how to be.

She didn't learn it from a book
She never needed any answers
She swore she'd never look
When he requested her to dance.

She never asked for sun or rain
She never wanted to numb the pain
No direction or change of pace
Wandered aimlessly behind an anonymous face.

Held strong her puppet strings
She played everyone else's role
She never lived life for her
The life she led was stole.

There was never time for herself
Never a chance for love
As she wounded this planet alone,
She never once looked above!

Charlene Soan

ARRIVED AT LAST

With rolled up sleeves they went to work
No task too hard they did not shirk,
Off comes the paper down came the timber
Such single mindedness I cannot remember.

The coffee shop needed a fresh facelift
So many items experience a shift,
It had not been used for many a day
But at last the project was under way.

The gospel will be preached and we will sing
And Margaret will bash her tambourine with a ting-a-ling-ling,
Passers-by will think we have lost our marbles
You should see us dance and try to warble.

When the basket comes round we will give most freely
Because we have been blessed we will not act meanly
The sermon is good and we listen intently
Now to put into practice the message instantly.

At the end of the meeting there's coffee, tea and biscuits
As we fellowship together we feel rather frisky,
What time is it now I shall have to dash
I have left the oven on full it will be burnt to an ash.

J V Waby

THE CHURCH THAT MOVED

In nineteen-thirty, down in the city
Stood an empty church, which was rather a pity
Due to come down, there was no other way
Until some 'uphill' people had their say

We'll move it up north, onto holy ground
To a site on St Gills that we have found
Would it be possible, you just have to ask
To achieve such an improbable task?

The people were keen and eager to start
Ferrying the stones by lorry and cart
For four long years the work went so well
A beautiful church arose from the shell

For many long years its ancient clock
Had ceased to tick - and also to tock!
The gears were all rusty and couldn't be wound
A more modern system just had to be found

An expert was called and he had to declare
Eight thousand pounds - the cost to repair
'That's a lot of money,' the locals were told
For modern machinery to replace the old

Head-shaving and dances, events there were many
Working so hard to raise every penny
With local support from The Echo at night
Reaching the total came into sight

Restoring the hands and face was one of the jobs
And a perspex cover to stop vandals and 'yobs'
So good luck to St Giles and all of the flock
Thanks for restoring your beautiful clock!

Doug Sheppard

The Writer's Journey

Explore with me, the writer's life.
A journey through my soul.
Without my words I'm nothing,
It's prose that makes me whole.

It starts with one short sentence,
The words and I are one,
And like a child with faltering steps,
The journey is begun.

In toddler years, I often fall
With tantrums by the score.
I wail at each rejection
And then I write some more.

As each experience shapes new life,
Committed to the page,
I paint my world with colours,
Of love and fear and rage.

The rocky teens, I'm racked with angst,
Low worth and self-esteem.
No longer sure I'll make the grade,
I'm braced to lose my dream.

My adult heart screams, 'Don't give up!
A writer you must be!'
And as my words turn into print,
The journey sets me free.

Beverley J Todd

BE GRATEFUL

From time to time we all get in unpleasant situations,
Even saints and millionaires have frequent irritations.
But all life's slings and arrows can be dealt with if you try
To hang on to this happy thought: the fact that dogs can't fly.

If your hair you pull when the bus is full and you're refused a place,
And the air turns blue when you're in a queue and feel it's a disgrace,
Please curb your temper if you can, just smile and heave a sigh
Remember what a wonderful thing it is that dogs just cannot fly.

If you think it's a sin when you feel your chin and find you've missed
a bristle or on a picnic in a field sit down upon a thistle,
While pulling thorns from your backside and a tear comes to your eye
Forget the pain; here's a thought to retain: thank Heavens
dogs can't fly.

If you're a dedicated soccer fan and your team's been relegated,
Or in the office find with paperwork you're inundated,
When you get home and a fuse has blown and you can't discover why,
Take my advice, and think how nice it is that dogs can't fly.

When jammed in a lift or cast adrift in a small boat out at sea,
If slugs have attacked your lettuce plants and the cat's stuck up a tree.
Don't be too sad, life's not so bad, let's be grateful, you and I,
That our canine friends have never had the wherewithal to fly.

If you've spent your pay at a takeaway, then trip and drop your pasty,
Or on the street in sandaled feet you step in something nasty,
When the whole mess goes between your toes, and makes you
want to cry
Though it may seem bad, be very glad dogs aren't equipped to fly.

If you're depressed or feeling stressed, then dwell on happier things,
For instance, we've been blessed with thumbs while dogs are lacking wings.
Imagine what a mess there'd be if hurtling from the sky,
Came a bomber squadron raid composed of dogs who'd learned to fly.

Lois Taylor

THE CUCKOO

In April the cuckoo comes to us
They settle down without much fuss.
The month of May they start to sing
To hear them is a wondrous thing.

The cuckoo never builds a nest
They depend on all the rest.
In some other nest they lay
Their eggs they stow, then fly away.

Some other bird brings up their young
Even though they don't belong.
They teach them how to feed and fly,
I wonder if they wonder, why.

And in the summer month of June
The cuckoo they doth change their tune.
A shortened version of their song
Their departure will not be long.

July is here it's time to go
All the young ones now in tow.
They don't stay long upon our shore.
To Africa, back home once more.

Susan Roden

A Gem Of A County

Beauty is in the eye of the beholder you may agree
So, this royal county's charms are there for all to see.
Go in any direction be it downs, meadows, river or lake
One can observe that the scenery is yours to take.
Look at the towns that this county can sustain
Visit any one they are there to sample and there for your gain.
Sonning, Windsor, Eton and Maidenhead is where Thames does flow
Some make it a pilgrimage and to these spots they go.
Industries of all kinds in Berkshire are found
Their products throughout the world abound.
So let us therefore reflect and sing-out aloud
That this royal county's beauty will forever remain a silver lining
                                            in every cloud.

Peter Parbery

Hope

Empty places, lonely faces
A world filled with grief
Everyone wishing for something
To bring them some relief
Many ask the question
Why must this be?
Will we ever have the answer?
Who is it that holds the key?
Love is the answer I've heard it said before
The more love I have to give
The more difficult is my life to live
So what am I doing wrong in my life of doom?
Do I just get on with it and clean another room?
And will the black cloud soon pass by?
So I can live my life, with no more stress and unhappiness
At least before I die.

Chris Needley

To Bare... Or Not

They wondered through the golden sands,
Where skies were cobalt-blue,
She stood and watched her two best friends
Then wondered what to do?

One by one they shed their clothes,
How could they be so brave?
'What possessed me,' Goodness knows!
Could dignity be saved?

First their T-shirts - then the jeans,
Would they bare their all?
Though on the beach - such sights were seen -
Some skinny - fat or tall.

Brassiers were strewn about . . .
Knickers - shorts and g-strings.
They've certainly got some guts, she thought,
Imagine - if a bee stings.

She just stood and watched and froze -
As they smeared on the suncream.
Shall I join them? Yes - here goes -
I'll have to do it sometime.

But then she thought - *it feels too rude,*
The weather's much too cold.
I cannot sunbathe in the nude,
I think I'm much too old.

Anyway - there's men about,
It doesn't seem quite right,
Although they're handsome hunks - no doubt -
I'd give them all a fright.

Wendy Watkin

SCENTS

A weathered skin and charred dry touch
keep senses locked in tightly.
There is no sight, no taste, too much
as steps they creep on blindly.

Lost panting feet, fed by the life
run from a past that's hurried.
Frail shaking bones and blighted strife
keep demons taught and buried.

Look to the sky, the empty space
a ceiling painted brightly.
It beckons hope out from the race
away from those less kindly.

Catch scented smells of ruined grass
a walk away from pleasure.
Seem dreams well-flogged and people dark
aghast at no more treasure.

So awake and feel the inner sense
the kindness wrapped up tightly.
It slows the day and speeds the night
that pesters us not sprightly.

It's waiting there, the unfolding dream
sweet calls of birds and sunlight.
The days grow long, a life well-stretched
the past, a lost leaden might.

Nigel Sinkins

AN OPEN EYE

Eyes that open to watch the world go round,
Ears that listen to hear the strangest sounds,
A simple touch that can make the day,
A beautiful scent that diffuses away.
A word of warmth to enlighten the mind,
A shining smile of someone so kind,
A ray of sunshine sent from the sky,
A shining star that seems so high,
A window ledge to watch outside,
A thousand secrets that you have to hide,
A subtle breeze to refresh the skin,
A basic goal encourages the win,
A glimmer of hope the strangest wish,
The strongest hug yet the softest kiss.

A darkened day with shadows cast,
Baring no sunshine as it draws out fast,
The hollow heart the shallow eye,
No smile to laugh no tear to cry,
The brisk wind the circle of dust,
No one to love no one to trust,
A violent hand sworn to attack,
A rotten flower that won't come back,
No mind to care or even think,
Vicious meanings in just one blink,
A wild beast that aren't really there,
The tightest clutch that's there to harm,
A distorted feeling unable to calm.

Some of them love some of them hate,
People are strange and increasing in rate,
Some of them frown some of them smile,
Everyone's different not all worthwhile,
Some are careless some of them cry,
An unknown world is an open eye.

Rebecca Timothy

Rejection

Why does no one want me? What have I done wrong?
Have I insulted someone in a previous life?
Have I committed a sin against mankind
Or am I just a product of Adam's sin, or bad karma?

Why am I rejected when I have much to give? Take a chance on me
Is it because I'm male, because I'm old, because I'm ugly?
Is it because of where I live, or I don't live like you
Don't drive a car like you, think, vote like you? Different

Does anyone care about the unemployed? I do
The government says it does and strangles us with rules
A subclass of the unwashed and thieves, who don't want to work
Drug users, drug dealers, abusers of every kind, it's true

The unemployed are the lowest of the low, people who sign the dole
Give us more and more handouts, jobs are for someone else
Give us self-respect and a job with a living wage, a future
Not slave labour and two pounds fifty an hour, take it or leave it

Go on a course, send more CVs, apply for more jobs, anywhere
The better you're educated the better the job, b******t
You can't use the computer for this, the rules say so, so don't
You should be grateful to use our services, you're not, ungrateful

Go to the Job Centre, client adviser, girl with two GCEs, one catering
You're not trying to get work, take any job, prove you're looking
for work
Look at me as an example, example of what? Stop his dole
Take a job as a dishwasher, a porter, forget your degree, a job's a job

Depression, failure, rejection, it's a way of life, unemployed
Letter came today, no interview, wishing me luck, rejection
Want to take my girl out, no money, make my family proud, no job
Tell my friends I'm working, and not hear the silence when
I say unemployed

It's getting better, who says? The government, those in jobs, not I?
The mortgage rate's coming down, important if you have a mortgage,
I don't
The FT index is rising, what the hell is the FT index? Who cares, I don't
I want a job, a proper job, no more rejection, no more failure, a job

Another day dawns, the post hits the floor, letters for me, hope perhaps
Scared to open letters, hate rejection, depression, must open letters
More rejection, more wishing me luck, stuff luck give me a job
What's the point, no one cares, rejection is a way of life, rejection is
all there is

Robert Joseph Parks

WOMAN WITH CARROTS

Sitting on the four-fifty-two
Alton train, a woman who
Was sort of middle aged
Sat opposite busily engaged

Looking for something from a bag
Emerging triumphant with a mag
And a large carrot from a bunch
Which she proceeded to masticate and munch

With loud crunching which drowned out
The mobile phones round about
Then as she had the last bit
Suddenly she was struck by a fit

Of gentle but definite hiccups
Lasting several minutes - then whoops
She found another carrot and
Ate and chomped through that . . .

Antony Sheaman

FAREWELL TO LOVE

I used to dream how close we'd be in our maturing years
But all I ever seem to do is shed a million tears.
The times that should have pushed us close have pulled us far apart,
And I'm left with only sadness coming from a broken heart.

All I ever wanted was to spend my life with you,
To share the ups and downs and turn each grey sky into blue;
But all the ups have drifted by and downs replace each one.
I ask myself what happened, and who took away the sun?

Each day is spent with tears in dwellings where there should be smiles,
Whilst guilt pervades a mourning brow creased deeply by the trails.
There is no joy, no hope, to quell a helplessness inside . . .
I go, my love, with memories of your once happy bride.

Patricia Samuels

ANNIE'S DOOR

Trouble came to Annie's door
It shook her to the very core.
Robbed during the dark of night
Has given everyone a fright.

But this lady she's got style
It'll be back to normal, in a while.
The smell of bacon, the smell of toast
'The finest coffee' Annie's boast.

Customers support during these hard times
Soon will be forgot this rotten crime.
They'll come back from being down
All the staff will wear evening gowns.

Denise Shaw

CHANGING BY NATURE . . .

As the land prepares to change once more
Summer's over for another year
The dawn chorus we once woke to
We can no longer hear.

The birds we've known in months gone by
Fly off to lands so far away
As we welcome our friend the robin
Who for the winter is here to stay.

The foliage quickly changes
Leaving the tree which once stood so proud and tall
So bare and thin and rickety
Another victim of the fall!

As we're engulfed by rusty, golden browns
Soon there's no greenery left in sight
Sleepily, animals crawl into hibernation
Struggling to stay awake with all their might.

Winter will be upon us
Before we can say Jack Frost
And as the entry to a new one looms
Another year is lost.

Thrown into the archives
Of our cunning, corruptive minds
To be stored away as memories
That no one ever finds.

In this world to which we belong
Lies such beauty that's rarely seen
But if we continue to blindly ignore it
Life as we know it will simply become a faded, worn out dream!

Louise Webster

The Knock Out

Here it comes, the car in front!
Nowhere to go, a wall covered in snow!
To my left, a tractor draws close!
The brakes don't work, not on this icy road.

Here it comes, the car in front!
Nowhere to go, crash! Bang! My life a flash in the pan.
Dreams all gone, thoughts are none!
If only another day would come.

The bonnet's folded neat, just like a couple of ironed sheets.
My head goes a thump, on the back of the seat!
Sitting back the blood rushes, my eyes close!
Down I go falling into a moment's deep sleep.

There it is, the car in front!
Singing and whistling, hooting and tooting!
Speaking its last words, as its wings flap to and fro.
The storm it was, stood still.

Blue lights are flashing, speedily along.
Luckily I awakened, although I started shaking!
Thoughts of rage, surfaced within.
The price of life was too great, even for a silly mistake.

George Petrie

Arctic Underworld

Dropping into the freezing sea,
'neath the surface, a world of green,
fluorescent walls surrounding me,
ceiling of ice, an eerie scene.

Curious seals go gliding past,
the dark shape of a whale below,
sifting plankton, its mouth so vast,
soon it's gone with the ocean flow.

In the water, a secret world
of unknown species from the deep,
jellyfish, tentacles unfurled,
their sting would give me cause to weep.

Creatures surviving in the cold,
endlessly searching for a meal,
life forms evolved from times of old,
drift with the current, seem unreal.

My mind plays tricks as I grow numb,
I long to stay, but time's run out,
forgotten risks, I had to come
to see such wonders, without doubt.

Ann Odger

ONLY A GAME

I wish someone would tell me; I can never understand
Why, just kicking a ball about is something to commend.
The goalposts are so wide apart, the ball so very small,
There surely is no skill to kick between those posts that ball!
Why do those men who play that game get enormous sums of money
For doing nothing more than that? I think it peculiarly funny.

I wish someone would tell me why, when a player scores a goal
The others jump upon his back and instead of calling, 'Foul,'
They pummel one another, punch the air, dance around,
Hide their heads in their jerseys and fell him to the ground?
The referee blows his whistle and adds one to the score.
He's done what he's been paid to do. Just that and nothing more.

For the winner, the contest ended whatever the sport or game,
A trophy is presented with a bottle of champagne.
Why do they not drink toasts with this? Will someone please explain.
Why do they shake the bottle until the cork plops out,
Erupting in a frothle over everything round about?
They shout and laugh uproariously as if they'd done something fine.
It puzzles me. It's such a waste of energy and of wine.

Beatrice M Wilson

TO A FAERY-THORN SEEN IN A FIELD IN IRELAND

It broke the ripples on a golden field of oats,
Annulled the one-ness of a rolling sun-kissed sea -
An island left to harbour dream-ward boats
That searched fulfilment by the ancient faery-tree.

No scything storm, no soil-drenched furrowing prow
Had dared erase that haven's proffered hand
That lovers might, enchanted, whisper-vow
And beach upon its rapturous faery-strand.

Gardiner M Weir

Essex

'We're moving,' said my husband, 'not too far I hope,'
I'm London born and bred, in Essex I will cope,
With bags all packed, van overflowing,
We left the city, 'at last we're going,'
I felt at peace in this place, as if I'd just come home,
Wander-lust extinguished, no more was I to roam,
It was a new beginning and a lovely one at that,
My eyes and ears were open, in the garden where I sat,
This 'nature thing' surprised me, boy, was I in awe,
I'd missed so much in London, never noticed it before,
The birdsong in the morning, welcoming each day,
Glistening dew upon the grass, inviting me to stay,
I feel blessed and very lucky, that I have had this chance,
To experience 'natural wonders', look, you take a glance,
The village where I live, is called Ramsden Heath,
My coming home, my peace of mind, memories I'll always keep,
The 'Cockney' girl has grown, but remembers her beginnings,
It's Essex where she'll stay, and finish off her 'innings'.

Denise Ryan

Darkness

As come fold upon fold you melt house, park and land
In hand we succumb to your talons expand
Why something described as matt and thick
How never the moment you come ahh secret your trick
Needle the light that pricks your ever growing shadow
To someone lone you beat nothing but sorrow
Plenty your gaze here, and infinity above
Hide now we cower sleep though if we could.

Cassius James

A Meeting At The Cenotaph The Miracle At The River Kwai

Long years ago the blind man said
I walked among the 'living dead'
By railroad, river, jungle deep
I prayed the Lord my soul to keep
In camps of squalor and despair
Lay broken men with vacant stare,
Diseased and suffering unreprieved
Victims of a brutal creed.

It was here the miracle began
It rose within the hearts of man,
Men prayed for guidance, strength to cope
They had little else but faith and hope,
They shared their blessings ever small
In selfless deeds beyond recall.

Skilled hand would soothe
Soft voices speak, the strengthened
Ministered the weak,
More bravely shed the ductless tear
Or stayed the trembling hand of fear,
In the survival of another
Brother gave his life for brother.

I could see the misted tears of pain
As his memory stirred his mind again
Then he quoted softly word for word
An epitaph not long since heard.

When you go home
Tell them of us and say
For your tomorrow
We gave our today

I did not fully understand
Why I took the blind man by the hand,
Yet I had the strangest sense of joy
I neither knew or reasoned why.
The glorious dead, peace, liberty,
The spirit of my heart was free.

June Pledger

TURNING CLOCKS BACK!

Wishing to change things for better
We cry to turn back time.
When, you know, even if we could,
Nothing would fall into line!
We would live out that exact same life
And make the same old mistakes
And once again have or cause
The exact same, sad old heartaches!
To change things, we would need to take
Back in time along with us,
All the stored memories we have today
Before from experience, we could heed!
Knowledge and experience of present life
Is key to change, in itself
For it grants foresight and wisdom.
Like a second set of eyes.
So rather than wish to turn back time
When your life seems in subsidence
Use past experience to put things right
Use past errors and mistakes as guidance!

C R Slater

A Summer's Day

It's a peaceful and tranquil day,
arms and legs bare, and on the ground I lay.
The sun beats down and warms my skin,
time to forget all my worries and sins,
then scornful and bitter a wasp dives down,
the devil of all insects came without a sound,
I jump up and down to scare him away
but he doesn't go away.
He is determined and chases me,
across the garden and into a tree,
As still as the tree he lands on my face,
we both know it's no longer a race,
for he takes his time to inspect me,
to find the perfect spot to be.
Do I squash him or give in,
either way he's going to win,
his stinger is out and about to imbed,
so I brush him off and kill him dead.
No longer a peaceful and tranquil day
but a stressful time in every way.
I pick up my blanket and go inside,
thinking, *I'm glad that wasp died.*

Tracey Stanton

THE GENESIS STORY

Glory, glory, glory: the Lord made Monday.
Let me tell you of the Genesis story.
How He came to make this world, fair Earth.
On the first day wisely, he decided,
To separate the black night from the light of day.
Made the warming sun and a swarm of stars.
Created the pallid, inconstant moon for Monday.
Come Tuesday, He used the second day,
To divide the land and the mighty waters,
The sunshine brought forth frothing clouds.
Then the Lord, clapped His hands in satisfaction.
Creating awe-inspiring thunder and lightning,
And the first cool, refreshing rain.
Without delay arrived Wednesday,
The Lord in His magician's robes, produced,
A cornucopia of grasses, fruit and flowers.
Nurtured by sunshine and frequent showers.
God saw Earth, as a park in all its blooming glory.
Saw it flourishing under his goodly husbandry,
The world on Thursday and Friday, decidedly more lively.
As He filled the Earth, with diverse fish and beasts.
Into the fragrant air, birds and bats He released.
At last came Saturday, to Him His best day.
He created in His own image, the man-creature Adam,
With His bride, Eve who some perceive as the temptress.
Then on the Sunday, God weary He took His rest.
Allowed the devil, as a spiteful viper, to tempt Eve,
As He lay abed sleeping, a dragon-form creeping.
Eve confessed to God of her misdemeanour,
The foolish pair cast from Eden's pleasure garden.

Jonathan Pegg

BY CHANCE

Like a meteor in the night
You pierced my heart with sharp delight
Like a rumour from the east
Unnerved me to a fierce unrest.

One afternoon of wind and rain
You came, by chance, to my poor room
Circled your skirt upon the floor
And tricked oblivion.

So learned my hopes to sing
At whisper of your name,
Winds of a wild romance
Fanned my dry heart aflame.

Hopeless, masochistic pain
That loving you, you'd love again
I dreamed, and dreamed in vain.
Fate played a shifty game
That summer long; puffed out my flame
And choked my song.

You went your way. Since when
When I come home
A handful of dry words upon a page
Is all I own.

Ray Racy

Someone, I Wish

To someone, I wish could be mine
Much more than a valentine
More than red roses
Or hearts on a card
Someone I think of
In high regard

To someone, I wish could be mine
Who outshines, the summer sunshine
More than silver
Much more than gold
Someone to be near to
I just want to hold

To someone, I wish could be mine
Who I could be with, all the time
More than this
My whole life long
Can being together
Be so wrong?

To someone, I wish could be mine
I mean every word, every line
More than this verse
Which I've written for you
All of which
Is all very true

B Page

TAKE ME!

Take my hand and lead me onwards,
with my heart, you'll take my love.
Release my soul, take it, free me,
into eternal clouds above.

I'll follow when you lead me,
my heart pierced with a sword,
I'll love you as you need me,
my life and soul forever yours.

Wrap your arms around my body,
make me safe within my soul.
I feel you close, inside my heart,
I can't give in , I won't let go.

I see reflections in the mirror,
but the real you, you're not here.
If you break this heart of mine,
it will shatter and shards as spears,

They'll pierce my love,
my heart will bleed.
I need your love to free me,
to follow, your hand I need.

Take my love and need me,
take my hand and lead me,
take my heart and love me,
my soul forever free.

Nikki Raven

LOVE REUNITED

How bright shines the moon
Making it seem morn came too soon,
As I walk down the street
My body feels light, my feet fleet.
I am going to meet my lover
So I am sparkling all over,
With the love, I will be able to say,
Hoping he still feels the same way.
As I reach our chosen destination
We'll be meeting at the station,
Where first we said our goodbye
As the train took him, perhaps to die.
Seeing a redhead in the distance
I rush faster, my feet do dance,
Suddenly he is there, eyes shining,
We embrace, my heart stops pining.
We hugged and we kissed
Feeling never to have missed
Each other's so loving heart,
Beating, knowing we need never part.

Marj Busby

ANYONE CAN WRITE POETRY

My father used to say to me,
When I was young and impressionable.
The engineer, self taught,
'I could do it if I wanted to,' he said.
But now, when he is gone and I am sixty,
I realise he said it because
He didn't understand me.
I have the soul of a poet and he
The soul of a mathematician.
Later he said he was proud when I was published.
But it took the bloom off the lily
Whenever I recalled those words uttered
When I was just twelve years old.
'Anyone can write poetry.'
He was wrong. My mother and I write poetry,
He couldn't.

Patricia Adele Draper

ADVERSITY

Do you think I can't hear you laugh,
as you pass me on the street?
Don't you think it hurts me,
to know you have me beat?
I may be a little different than you,
on the outside, that is all,
but still, I hear you snigger,
and the names you need to call.
I hope it makes you feel good,
to think you are better than me,
even though, inside, we are the same,
a heart like mine, you'll never see.

Michelle Rae

AUTUMN REVELATION

The fallen leaves that spun in leaps
and bounds at every chattering gust
now lie trapped in rustling heaps
or whirl about as drifting dust.

These leaves that once the sound
of wind moved in whispering green
revealed those birds that found
cover in their shifting screen.

Lone in a park's soft summer shade
a single homeless man had found
some shelter - his bed he made
safe under bushes dry and sound.

Weeks into months he slept unseen
and squirrels peeped from drey
on sheltered form as the green
canopy thinned to brown and grey.

One November day as gentle breezes flayed
the leafy blanket off the man concealed
top deck bus commuters saw revealed
the curled up body in death decayed.

Anthony J Brady

I LOVE YOU STILL

So much bottled up inside
So many emotions I conceal
Do everything within my power to hide
These feelings must not be revealed
For they won't understand
That after all this time
I'm loving you
Still

Often without my volition
Memories of us seem to appear
I try and I try with everything I have
To shake them off to make them disappear
Because each time I reminisce I'm always reduced to tears
Can't talk to no one about it
They won't understand what I feel
How deep my love is for you
Still

They don't know how I felt when you looked into my eyes
Or how deep our love was as if we had soul ties
They haven't felt what it was like when you kissed
Every inch of my perfectly shaped lips
I felt so safe when wrapped in your arms
Never ever worried of being subjected to harm
We seemed to be so happy when we were together
A concept we adopted and promised to each other forever
Oh how much I miss you
How much my heart aches
That I'm separated from you another day
It hurts more so
That I can't tell a soul
Me still loving you they must not ever know
They won't understand how I feel
How much I love you
Still

I cry myself to sleep sometimes for my heart aches with pain
When I feel my tears start run free I seek comfort from the rain
For when I go and join my friend I don't have to abstain
From crying over what I feel 'cause my tears wash away with the rain
They said with time my feelings of loving you will go away, you'll see
On the contrary it only seems to have gotten deeper within me
The hardest part is keeping it secret, it mustn't be revealed
What my lonesome heart feels
Because they won't understand
How I could love you
Still

Tonya M Barber

INVISIBLE MAN

He died a lonely man!
The man on the street, who lived alone.
He used to say he enjoyed the peace,
The king of the castle, without a throne.

He lived a lonely life!
The man on the street with the see-through face.
He said he never needed a sole,
Though he would shed a tear in his quiet place.

He said a belated prayer!
The man on the street who left it too late.
You could see fear in his eyes,
He never prayed to God, do you believe in fate?

I miss the lonely man!
The man on the street with a heart of gold.
I see his timid eyes,
The invisible man who will never grow old.

Peter Wesley Hayward

POPPIES

The blood red poppies
Sway in the autumnal breeze
The day is calm,
Destruction has ceased.
It is silent
Only birdsong fills the air
There is nothing wrong,
No reason to care.
But at a time
There was death and hurt,
Pain and sorrow,
Noise and dirt.
It is hard to believe,
A thought so hard to conceive
That this barren scenery was
Filled with anxiety and despair
Many years have passed
The grassy banks in the distance grow bare
As the blood red coloured poppies
Sway in the autumnal breeze.

Stephanie Pereira

WHEN I WRITE

I don't always write when I'm happy
It's sometimes when I'm sad.
Things aren't always that good,
Sometimes it's really quite bad.

Grandad isn't here anymore
Cancer took him away.
Mum gets upset and cries,
I really don't know what to say.

Friends aren't always that nice,
Sometimes they make me feel full of ice.
Mum always knows what's inside my head,
She always knows when something nasty is said.

She hugs me and kisses me
To make me feel better.
I hold her and hug her
And it works so I let her.

Sian Marie Mernor

SINGLE ROSE

I have placed before you, an invisible red rose,
though it has no soft sweet smelling fragrance,
so as for you to speak of.
But it may in that way therefore,
flourish and remain for eternity.

Cindy Cross

DAEMON FLU

It's no ordinary flu;
This daemon flu;
When you're old,
If it settles on you,
A sniffle - a cough;
Your skin feels hot,
A tipple you'd scoff,
Rather rot!
Aches and pain;
Limb to limb;
Inside your brain;
Feel so grim,
Throat like gravel;
Rasping bark;
Down to your navel,
In the dark;

Dare not sleep,
Too long at a time;
In a deep
Sea of lime;
Daemons surging
Round your blood,
You keep floating,
In a sea of mud;
And sitting up,
Splitting head;
Drink this cup . . .
Rather be dead!
And so you rise
To get some air;
Hallucinatory lies
As down they stare;

This drug you're taking,
Fleming's way,
Has the making,
To send us away;
But if you are . . .
Mark this phrase,
You've made your share
Of enemies;
You may well rail,
Your reckless way;
Hornet's tail
Now you pay!

I may not splash
A heavy stone;
Nor will I trash,
Who are my own;
As Hamlet said,
In his soliloquy;
Father dead,
Mother free,
When I get up,
Conscience - fear,
Your daemon cup,
Your mutant spear;
A coward - am I,
Like other men,
Before I die,
Have this drug again . . .

Tom Ritchie

Farewell

May all you wish for come your way
your lives be long and sweet.
May happiness and good fortune
be found on every street.
I pray you find the happiness
that you've been searching for.
A life that's full of plenty
Success, and so much more.
May this be the first step that
puts you firmly on your feet.
And this be the journey that
makes your life complete.
And if you find a moment
to spare a thought or two,
For all the ones you've left
behind who still think of you.

Irene Keeling

Old Mother Earth

'Come in, please take a seat
At last we finally meet,
Your test results have just come back
I cannot lie, the outlook is black.
You have contracted a nasty infection
Commonly known as human population,
What it is doing, Mrs Earth
Is stripping you, of all your worth.
Like a cancer spreading to your core
Unfortunately, with no apparent cure,
We can only hope it starts to care
About you and your atmosphere.'

A C Small

HOW WE LIVED

Wipe the window, and the door,
Do the potatoes after the floor.
Beat the rug before you put it back
And put way the vegetable rack.
Did you put back my seat?
Go to the butcher's for the meat.
Get a bone for the dogs,
When you come back get the logs.
All this before I went to school,
The kids treated me as a fool.
I just managed to slip into line,
Just as the bell rings it's nine.
Oh I feel such a real ninny,
I forgot to take off my pinny.
So I'm told to leave the hall,
Had to stand near the wall.
Told to put my apron away,
I was not allowed to go to play.
You was taught not to interrupt,
That's the way we were brought up.
My hard days and teaching I don't regret,
And my up-bringing I'll never forget.
Yes they were strict, we were poor,
They taught us how to live within the law.

Margaret Upson

DESOLATION PLANET EARTH

It is the year 2120,
I am Kryaux, an interplanetary voyager,
From beyond the boundaries of time,
My destination planet Earth,
Tales of a once-wondrous planet,
In a far-off solar system set me upon this journey,
Once Gaia was held in high esteem,
A jewel amongst planets,

Exquisite,
Is how early pioneers of your universe described it,
An oasis of lush and green vegetation,
And crystal clear oceans,
A vast and incredible variety of life-forms,
Inhabited both land and sea,
After aeons an intelligent species,
Homo-sapiens evolved,

These were custodians of the planet,
Yet over time they created chaos,
And turned it into a desolate wilderness,
Adrift in the celestial heavens,
Wars erupted brother against brother,
Destructive killing machines,
Rendered the Earth stained with their blood,
Pollution on land and sea choked its nucleus,

From sagas handed down on my home world,
It is said to be now only a lifeless sphere,
Around which an impenetrable ochre atmosphere hangs,
The crew and myself are pioneers from the future,
Who have travelled via a time barrier many light years,
Our mission is to endeavour to create an environment,
Using our advanced technology,
Where life once more can inhabit planet Earth.

Ann G Wallace

ALL GROWN UP

Birthday boy, now you are six,
A pirate bouncy castle and caravan ship,
Hope you are all fit,
Everyone will do their bit,
Pirate theme is what you requested,
Pirate theme is what you were blessed with.

A decorated caravan with birthday banners and flags
Cake and ice cream and party loot bags,
All your friends came and had a good play,
We were lucky with the weather, sunny all day.

The presents you were given were greatly received,
Underneath you were very secretly pleased
Whispering to everyone near,
It will be just as good again, if I know my mum, next year.

Your friends came to share your big day,
Bringing presents galore, they had lots to say,
They played and jumped on the pirate ship
Until they were sore, could not stand, just slip.

The balloons were rockets that screamed through the air,
Party poppers that showered tinsel down into your hair.
A pirate treasure hunt rounded off the day and
When home time came everyone wanted to stay.

All good things come to an end,
Maybe this is hard to comprehend but
The memory stays with us all,
A party to remember, a young boy named *Luke* standing tall.

Jill K Gilbert

THE KNOWLEDGE

This morning as I went into the room, I knew.
This morning as I gazed at your face, I knew.
This morning as you nuzzled my hand, I knew.
No need for doubts, time was right I knew.

Your thin creaky legs ached, I knew.
Your glazed old eyes blind, I knew.
Your droopy silver ears deaf, I knew.
No need for regrets, time was right I knew.

Playing with your toys no more, I knew.
Pulling on the lead no more, I knew.
Panting as breath you fight, I knew.
No need for fear, time was right I knew.

As I carried you to the place, I knew.
As I lay you on the table, I knew.
As you closed your eyes, I knew.
No need for tears, now peace you know.

Lorraine Noble

DAUGHTERS

Daughters are such precious things,
I cannot explain the happiness they bring.
Just to see them every day,
Chases all my sadness away.
A breath of spring air they are to me,
To my heart they hold the key.
No tears do I ever see, no it's always laughter and glee.
My daughters are so beautiful and pure
And that's how I aim to keep them
And that's for sure.

J T Lister

A Forest Glade

A forest glade on a summer's day,
In sunbeams see rabbits and squirrels play,
A vixen with her cubs to pass,
A doe with her fawns graze on forest grass.

Above the sound of a woodpecker tapping,
A jay to screech, pigeon wings flapping.
A woodcock to call in alarm,
What could there be, to cause any harm?

High above a sparrow hawk hovers,
Its keen eyes, acres it covers,
Little to move without it seeing,
On the ground every little being.

Sun's warmth to penetrate deep,
Into Mother Earth, energy seep.
Where damp the dew of early morn,
Now dry, moisture been drawn.

Who sees this tranquil charm
Or feels such wonders of natural calm?
These things are for all to see.
If, at one with nature, you're willing to be.

Alan Morgan

TERRIBLE TWOS

Oh it's hard being a two-year-old
    There are things you want but *'No'* you're told
There's not enough hours in the day
    To learn all the words they expect you to say

I've done so well up to this time
    I've learnt what's theirs and what's mine
I've used my legs and learned to walk
    I've listened hard and learned to talk

I've learned to count from one to ten
    And then I say it all again
I hear them say that I'm so bright
    Cos I know my colours black, red or white

And so what will next year bring?
    Playschool; I'll be expected to sing
Expected to share all the toys
    With lots of other girls and boys

I'll play with water, and things like sand
    Oh I can't wait it will be grand
I'll learn to tie up my laces
    And run like mad to win the races

I'll do a picture with the paint
    And Mum will say I'm a little saint
It'll be of me all thin and tall
    And Mum will hang it on the wall

Then in the year that I am five
    I'll be so glad to be alive
I'll be learning all day till four
    Then bring it home and learn some more

I'll learn to read and learn to write
    I'll even learn to fly my kite
All the words I'll learn to spell
    And they will say I've done so well

Then in the year that I am six
    There'll be another box of tricks
I'll learn to swim without a float
    And button up my overcoat

Then when I'm in size thirteen boots
    I'll wear long trousers or even suits
And just when I think I've learnt it all
    I'll learn to throw and catch a ball

That's when, at last I'll learn my friend
    To all this learning there'll be *no end.*

L Fritchley

LADY MOON

Orange orange deepest orange
In the dark dark midnight sky
I watch my lady moon on her
Back with her nose in the air
Draped in a colour only she dare wear

Why I wonder at this odd choice
I have heard about her dressed in blue
And have seen her silver gown
But there she is for all to see
Over country village, moor or town
Orange orange deepest orange
In the dark dark midnight sky

Pauline Stevens

MINE EYES

As I look into the skies
The wheels catch mine eyes
Spitting out rays, of the sun.
I can still hear men talking
As we often went a walking
To the dark days of work, we done.

As I look into the skies
The tears fill mine eyes
For all the workmates, I knew.
Though some in the hereafter
I can still hear jokes of laughter
Maybe I can share some, with you.

As I look into the skies
I sometimes wonder why
We toiled away, from the sun.
For now I spend time yearning
And wished that we'd been earning
In a daylight world, full of fun.

As I look into the skies
Mine eyes are full of pride
Now I drink a toast to recall
That you never take for granted
Good times where all we wanted
Here's to my mates, one and all.

John Henry Stafford

GOLDEN

A golden day, a golden year,
My heart is full of cheer.
Fifty years of joy and tears,
Fifty years of happiness and fears.
If I had to do it all again,
To share the joy and endure the pain,
Days of sunshine and of rain
And I look back at those golden days,
And even after all those years
Our love is still as golden now
As it was in those days when we were
Young and time flew by.

I see the love-light in your eyes,
The golden light of yesteryears,
Is still as sweet and still as tender
That all I can do is to remember
And thank the Lord above for those
Golden days of love.

Joyce Lawrence

MY SINGLE BEAUTIFUL ROSE

The tiny red rose peeps from under a leaf
I can hardly see my rose, is it hiding underneath?
There are no more buds only one little rose
It's there for my mum, and she always knows
Mum has gone away, I want to know why
The special rose was always her pride and joy
I have looked after the rose for many a year
I have this rose I know my mum is near
I think about her so much day and night
The rose brings us together in the fading light

I will always care for the rose for myself and my mum
I cannot share the rose with just anyone
Once the rose was picked, pressed and saved
I can open my book to see it on winter days
Only one rosebud grows every year
Replacing the rose that always appeared

Until then Mum, the rose is with us forever
I will always remember you and forget you never
I remember well the good times we always had
There were many happy moments and not many sad

Another years comes and the rose appears
It helps to see it when I shed many tears

Jenny Plant

CATCH ME IF YOU CAN

Poets have striven to catch me;
But how to capture a lark's song
bursting on the ear with mere
simile, metaphor, rhyme . . .
or convey a rousing waltz in time
to the rhythm of a spring breeze
playing for the coming again
of all things bright and beautiful,
all creatures, great and small?

Painters have striven to catch me;
But how to capture the blue of a sky
on a summer's day, or its hues
of red and gold at the sun's setting
on a glorious reawakening
to the beauty of life, for all its ups
and downs, treasures lost and found,
hopes dashed, sure to be recovered
if only we look long and hard?

Musicians claim to have caught me
in an embrace of song whose beauty
must surely equal the sweet lay
of a nightingale at the closing of day
seen all that's best in man and beast,
the worst forgotten, let fade away
like blood stains in a weeping sky
spelling out the names of those
among us sure to die

Dearer by far than all we own
is love's setting, not its stone

R N Taber

SUCCESS

Success is something, we all aim for,
Be it mental, physical, or a just reward,
An achievement, or an effort, so wisely thought
From past generations, lessons well taught.

Relief from misery, of unexplained pain
Where every effort, is not fought in vain
A sigh of relief, when back to normal, well being
Knowing success as achieved, and fought willingly.

Success, in all our physical strength, and might
Competing with other nations, for success in sight
Rewarding with team work, an effortless plight
To achieve a just ovation, and well deserved right.

So success in all things, love, life and laughter,
Not forgetting the effort, to gain a reward after.
The wonderful feeling of success with such might
Gives life worth living, a rewarding fight

But success is not always, what it seems to be
Unless, deep in your heart, your conscious is free
Knowing that the success, that has been gained
Deserves that medal, a proud achievement to remain.

C King

CELEBRITY HOTEL

Stands a history high within the making
It used to be the highlight of every subject
Only overshadowed with neglect
Stood a hero for his cause
Only envy gave no applause
When building along the finest coast
He finally did come the host
The finest building upon the land
Even gave back his people
More than a helping hand
Others came and betrayed his trust
They only made a lot of fuss
Within their ignorance he prevailed
Given determination he never failed
Determined within his will
He always paid the final bill
Only to be dwarfed within his tracks
Others would only want to attack
Now stands a location
Awaiting all to take that vacation
The scenery well set
The inhabitants they haven't met
Given time and unity
This hotel holds a great opportunity!

Suzan Gumush

BIG STRONG BOYS

'Would you like to paint my grandad clock?'
To the big strong boys I said
'And how about some MDF
At the top of my antique bed
Paint my parquet floor for me a lovely brilliant white
I will leave it up to you - are you sure it will look right?
Take my Adam furniture to the tip
Sling my Persian carpets in the skip
Throw away my crystal chandelier
Maintaining that is far too dear
Don't forget my Constables and my Dhalis too
Take them to a charity shop
They are worth a bob or two
Do some modern art for me to hang upon my wall
A bit of a doodle on hardboard
To show visitors when they call
Remove the brass handles from my doors
Put plastic ones in their place
I always thought those expensive ones
Looked rather a disgrace
Rip my brand new kitchen out I never liked it much
Put some MDF on the surfaces
The marble was so cold to touch
Paint my washer a really nice green
Paint my microwave too that should compliment the scene
When you paint all my kitchen tiles blue
How about painting my new fridge red?
You will find a new can in the shed
How long do you think before the jobs are done?
All in a day - well that's good Son
I suppose I could sleep in my MDF bed
But I may just stay at Mother's instead
No disrespect, it looks alright
But how do I clean a floor painted white?

I have three big strong boys of my own
A muddy dog who likes to roam
They all come in with muddy boots too
Will not take them off like some folks do
Oh! Me oh my the paint will scratch
When one too many goes down the hatch
And what about the spillages on my floor so white?
I think I will have to clean the lot morning, noon and night
So thank you boys, a job well done
I am glad you came to call
But when my husband sees it he may just go up the wall.'

E Dunn

'DIE' HEAT

The sun is hot the grass is dry
I watched the plants and flowers die
A cloud above moved slowly on
Until it dimmed the burning sun
The sky grew dark the cloud moved on
And once again the burning sun
The Earth cracked slowly 'neath my feet
A lone bird searched the dried up lake
A bead of sweat fell from my brow
I wondered why - I wandered how!
A withered leaf fell to the ground
Silently - without a sound
Distant thunder rumbled by
A flash of lightning streaked the sky
I waited for the rain to come
It didn't rain the storm moved on
I looked towards a scorching sky
And then I laid me down to die

Gloria B Rogers

WHY AM I HERE?

Why am I here?
I don't remember you.
This isn't my home.
It's dark in here, too.
At night I'm afraid
And I feel alone,
I have nothing
To call my own,
My children don't come,
They're busy, you see,
I hate it here,
Why do you stare at me?
I sit here thinking
Of the way
I used to love living
Every day,
But now it's different,
I can't think clear,
I don't remember you,
Why am I here?

Marion Schoeberlein

HE WALKS WITH ME

He walks with me like my shadow
He guides me when the paths diverge
He shines a light in my darkness
He brings a fire to my cold

His hand reaches for me when I fall
His eyes catch mine and bring me laughter
His strength keeps me going when I am tired
His wisdom brings my dreams to reality

I hear his voice when all seems lost
I feel his warmth in times of need
I call his name when fear surrounds me
I feel him close when I need him the most

Sam Ambrose

ANOTHER VIETNAM

As one man sleeps in his lonely grave
Others try desperately to save
Their own precious reputation
Deluding themselves and fooling the nation
'We did nothing wrong!'
Where have I heard that song before?
Vietnam? That crazy war?
'What *are* we fighting for?'
Don't ask me! I don't give a damn!
It's just another Vietnam!
$43 billion the cost of the war
And *we* will be paying for evermore

S Farley

BE STILL

How often do we look
But never see
The power of the eagle
And beauty of the tree.

The blind man sees
More in his day
Because he feels
And listens on his way.

A raindrop on the leaf
Like jewels in the sun
Dew in the morning
And when the day is done.

The smell of hedgerows
After the rain
Birds as they sing
The sound of the train.

Children playing in the
Distance, without a care
Shouting to one another
Their sound floating on the air.

Be still!
Realise, the peace and
Tranquillity of the moment
For it will never come again.

We can never experience
This time again
However much we try
Only the memories remain.

All we have is here and now!

Joan May Wills

IT'S MY LIFE

It's my life
And I'll lead it how I choose
It's my life
I don't want no one to refuse
It's my life
I want to forget about the past
It's my life
There ain't no shadow cast

It's my life
I'll get what I deserve
It's my life
It's all a learning curve
It's my life
I'll give it all I've got
It's my life
I've only got one shot

The life I led before
Had only one ray of hope
And all I have is my dream
Of getting that hope back.

People say that dreams don't come true,
But I know in time, they always do
Just believe in your thoughts and one day
You'll get exactly what you deserve and fly away.

It's my life
I'll fight until my dying day
It's my life
I will win back the love I lost
It's my life
I just wanna live it my way
It's my life
I will believe and he will be mine.

J Stone

A Mother's Lament

Why did they take her, where did she go?
From out of some darkness, their evil aglow
They stole her in malice, intent to destroy
Heedless of pain, her body their toy.

Did they take her with a lust out of control?
Did they know what they were doing when her body they stole?
Sent from some hole into our light
Self gratification our lives to blight

Their breath surely stank, from the sewer they came
0Evil incarnate, loathsome with shame
Does the sight of our children innocently playing
Fill them with greed their souls decaying?

Why did they take her, was their evil intent?
The pain of my suffering to make them content
They stole her and killed her, destroying all hope
The anguish I feel - how will I cope?

Emma M Gascoyne

ANCHOR BOOKS
SUBMISSIONS INVITED
SOMETHING FOR EVERYONE

ANCHOR BOOKS GEN - Any subject, light-hearted clean fun, nothing unprintable please.

THE OPPOSITE SEX - Have your say on the opposite gender. Do they drive you mad or can we co-exist in harmony?

THE NATURAL WORLD - Are we destroying the world around us? What should we do to preserve the beauty and the future of our planet - you decide!

All poems no longer than 30 lines.
Always welcome! No fee!
Plus cash prizes to be won!

Mark your envelope (eg *The Natural World*)
And send to:
Anchor Books
Remus House, Coltsfoot Drive
Peterborough, PE2 9JX

**OVER £10,000 IN POETRY PRIZES
TO BE WON!**

Send an SAE for details on our latest competition!